Before healing with Tasha,
angry and frustrated. She
to drop into my emotional
reconnect to my own story ,
actually desire & how to market that in my content for my business. It was amazing how much she helped me both personally & professionally!

Kelly Chase,
Star of Netflix Love is Blind

I find it incredibly moving and a bit scary howTasha knows exactly what's in my heart, mind, body, and soul. I don't have to say anything out loud and she already knows what I'm thinking & going through. I'm blown away by how on point and gifted Tasha is & there are moments when I can't wait for my next reading.

Michael Costello,
International Celebrity Designer

Tasha is so warm and gives such great personal readings. Her abilities not only help with guidance but her energy is incredible!

Kariselle Snow,
Star of Netflix Perfect Match

The first time I worked with Tasha, it blew my mind. Not only has she been right about everything but it's like getting therapy & insight all in one. Not to mention she's a dope as hell friend & so so easy to talk to.

Amanza Smith ,
Star of Bravo's Selling Sunset

A CELEBRITY PSYCHIC'S GUIDE TO BECOMING UNF*CKWITHABLE

TASHA WALL

SPIRITUAL HOTNESS: a celebrity psychic's guide to becoming unf*ckwithable

To ensure privacy and confidentiality, the names and other identifying characteristics of the persons included in this book have been changed. All the personal examples of my own life and experiences have not been altered.

ISBN 978-1-961185-29-6 (hardcover)
ISBN 978-1-961185-32-6 (paperback)
ISBN 978-1-961185-34-0 (digital)

Editing, Formatting & Layout: Megs Thompson – megswrites llc
www.megswrites.com

www.inomniaparatuspublishing.com

spiritual hotness:

(ADJECTIVE)

A SENSE OF BEING DROP-DEAD GORGEOUS AF WHEN IT COMES TO A WOMAN'S MIND, BODY & SOUL; POSSESSING THE ABILITY & CONFIDENCE TO OWN & BALANCE YOUR INNER GOOD GIRL & INNER VILLAIN.

thirst trap:

(NOUN)

A STATEMENT OR PHOTOGRAPH THAT IS INTENDED TO ATTRACT ATTENTION; THE SHAMELESS EMBRACE OF ONE'S INNER SKANK; A WOMAN VILLAINIZED FOR SIMPLY OWNING HER BODY & UTILIZING IT TO STIR THE POT OR START A MOVEMENT.

unf*ckwithable:

(ADJECTIVE)

UNABLE TO BE FUCKED WITH; UNTOUCHABLE, IMPERVIOUS TO, OR UNDETERRED BY OPPOSITION.

INTENTIONS

Over the last year writing this book, I've watched so many miracles unfold in my life like a magical whirlwind of wishes, and dreams, and seeds that sprouted all along the way!! What I didn't expect was to completely transform while writing my story with the teachings that go alongside it. My intentions are, that by the time you reach the final chapter, you too will be a new woman, but not just any woman, one who will not be fucked with!

With this book, I solemnly declare that you will go for what you want, and you will not take no for an answer. I declare that you'll stand up for yourself, your dreams, your wants, and your needs with tenacity, grace, and ease. From this moment on, no matter what, you won't be even a teaspoon less than who you really are. You will read this book knowing that you can have, literally, exactly what you want in life, and you will not settle for taking any breadcrumbs of less.

You'll become the woman who keeps the promises you make to yourself, and you'll watch the magic unfold as you twerk it and work it along the way as needed, knowing who and what to let go of, and when. If someone pushes you so far that you need a moment to whip out your inner bitch, then you will do so with confidence and you will not apologize for one millisecond about it.

Now, right before we begin, I want you to create your own magic spell by closing your eyes saying out loud a wish for what you'd like to receive out of reading this book, and picture how it will feel when that wish comes true. With that, I declare an Amen chica! Go forth and be unf*ckwithable.

Let's dig in!

TABLE OF CONTENTS

FOREWORD

In the sacred journey of life, there are individuals who emanate a divine light, guiding others towards their true essence. Tasha is without a doubt one such innately talented individual. As a powerful healer, she walks this path with wisdom, humor, and a touch of her own spicy magic. Tasha, a radiant soul in the realm of healing and sensual activation, possesses extraordinary gifts that transcend the "norm. Tapping into her psychic prowess to act as a beacon of insight, piercing through the veils of the unseen with unparalleled clarity. As someone who's known and interacted with Tasha for multiple years, I've had the pleasure of observing her magical healing abilities over and over again, a true testament to the divine energy flowing through her, as she effortlessly transforms lives and nurtures the spirit.

As a weaver of dreams and a guardian of the mystical, Tasha embodies the essence of the divine feminine, embracing both the inner villain and spiritual goddess we each possess. Her personal journey is a dance between intuition and practicality, a balance that empowers those around her to embrace their own unique gifts without judgement, self-doubt, or hesitation. With an aura that resonates with equal parts strength and softness, Tasha invites others to embark on their own transformative journey of self and soul discovery to invoke the sensual connection between the mind, body, and soul. In the tapestry of healers, Tasha stands as a luminary, illuminating the path to awakening and TRUE embodiment.

Within these pages, Tasha delves into her own personal stories of growth, discovery, and hilarity, sharing teachings in hopes that you, the reader, are inspired by the magic she shares. Empowering you to be the catalyst for your own spiritual awakening. Her wisdom and quirky brand of comedy

are sure to rock your world, making you laugh out loud at her direct, blunt, open, loving, and raw magic. She never hesitates out of fear of being too much or not enough and is a shining star here to teach us how to thicken our skin so that we can continue on our own journey,
unfazed.

Echo Summer Hill
Spiritual Leader & Divine
Feminine Embodiment Mentor

Echo Summer Hill
Spiritual Leader & Divine
Feminine Embodiment Mento

INTRODUCTION

I THOUGHT I WAS GOD

"thirst trap (noun): a statement or photograph that is intended to attract attention; the shameless embrace of one's inner skank; a woman villainized for simply owning her body & utilizing it to stir the pot or start a movement

We've all heard the term "thirst trap" before, usually when we're chatting with girlfriends about a scandalous photo we saw posted online or a scantily dressed woman twerking on the bar. Thirst traps are those moments when a woman decides to embrace her inner skank and allow that little bit of villain in her to come out and play. To seek, demand, and get off on the attention she receives. The term thirst trap sometimes brings with it negative thoughts and feelings when in reality, thirst traps are nothing more than a way for us to get exactly what we want, faster and easier. It's instant gratification and validation in the form of likes, loves, comments, jaw drops, glares, stares, whispers, and the occasional insult. If we're being completely honest, I find it equally satisfying to get a rise out of people whether it be in the form of an insult or a compliment. It doesn't much matter what the reaction is, so long as it happens while I am simply existing and just allowing myself to be me. Thirst traps are a way for us, as women, to lead with our flaming hotness as the part of ourselves that we're most comfortable with and confident in. Allowing us to make an entrance, cause a scene, capture attention, and create waves with our jaw-dropping shock factor, before allowing people to really see the other, softer, more vulnerable, and often imperfect pieces of ourselves. Of course, we can always do the more mature thing and lead with our vulnerable authentic flawed selves, but it's so much more fun to test the waters by having a scandalous moment, shaking a butt

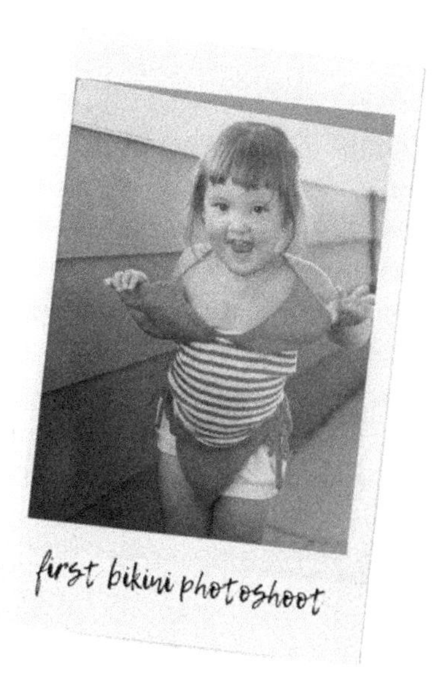
first bikini photoshoot

cheek, and popping a titty in someone's face, just to see what they'll do, before deciding to take the plunge and open up. What can I say, I like to have a real punch with my presence.

But we've got a whole book to dig into that, so let's get to know each other first since we'll be spending quite a bit of time together. Sit down and grab your favorite snacks because things are about to get real nitty gritty up in here.

I'm Tasha, a proud thirst-trapper, celebrity psychic and healer, and what I like to call, a self-made supermodel. I help to deliver and translate people's messages from the future most epic version of themselves to who they are today, so that they're able to begin building what I call our personal "stairway to heaven," healing anything inside you that is in the way of you becoming the supermodel star of your own show. You're probably wondering, *"What's that all mean?"* Well, it means my clients and I go deep, digging into the grimy inner work around their past breakups, fat gain, betrayal, motherhood, sex, anxiety, and everything that's stealing their sparkle, while also bringing all that depth, pain, happiness, and healing to the surface, creating actual, tangible, steps that form the building blocks and "stairway to heaven." Meaning your dream will no longer be dreams, they'll become your own real life, so much so that you'll be in awe and quite literally mind blown over what you always wished you could create and now have! This kind of healing shows up as toned abs, thigh gaps, stacked savings accounts, rolling orgasms, dream marriages, family vacations, skyrocketing careers, and a wardrobe that takes your breath away. I see so many women working on improving their hearts, bodies, emotions, and spirits, but never getting the actual physical results they want, leaving them feeling like everything is changing on the inside, but things aren't matching on the outside. Too often it can feel like we're working so damn hard on ourselves and our own evolution but being left with the same old dry vagina, underwhelming men, extra weight, and mediocre bank accounts. That's where I differ from other healers and psychics. My superpower is helping my clients to heal their shit so that they can experience the real-life results they want in their relationships with food, men, money, love, sex, and their career. I don't just sit there with my crystal ball predicting the future, I help you design the future you actually want.

You're probably wondering, *"But Tasha, how'd you become a celebrity healer and supermodel psychic?"* Great question. 12 years ago, while I was at the gym, running on the treadmill and watching the Victoria's Secret fashion show, I experienced my very first vision and "message." The images were clear as day, and I knew immediately who the message was meant for, but I wasn't entirely sure what the message meant. It was kind of like waking up one day and realizing I could speak Chinese, but not understanding what I was saying. Like I was saying the words, and speaking the language but feeling like I made absolutely no sense at all. However, I knew with certainty that the messages I was seeing, and what I was saying, were coming directly from God himself (or we can say herself if you prefer God to be a woman). Pretty quickly I started to receive consistent messages and downloads on demand for various clients and people in my life, which I now know and recognize as channeling. I felt in every piece of my puss, my core, and my very being that I was THE CHOSEN ONE. Basically, I felt like I was some sort of walking modern-day reincarnated version of Jesus himself, and I loudly and proudly wanted to share that with anyone who was willing to listen. I let them know without any hesitation that, "*I CAN TALK TO GOD*!!!"

I encouraged people to ask me anything they liked, and I'd deliver God's replies directly back to them because I was basically Jesus Christ reborn. The funniest part about this time in my life, is that everyone I shared my newfound gift with believed me because I so strongly believed it myself! I was so sold on myself and my newborn gifts as the chosen one, that most of the people I interacted with were flabbergasted and eager to hear all about what message I could deliver to them, I did however, have one "friend" who was convinced that I was losing myself, my grasp on reality, and hinted at the fact that I was becoming schizophrenic. Back then I didn't know how to deliver my channelings in a way that made sense to everyone, and as humans we can often become afraid and scared of things that we don't understand. My personal belief is that a lot of mental illnesses are misdiagnosed because people are unaware of how to use their spiritual gifts, and are tapping into different energetic planes, souls and energies, speaking to multiple channels and beings at once. I genuinely believe that every mental illness has a spiritual meaning and cause behind it, as well as countless other contributing factors like but "mental illnesses" are definitely not as simple as people just "going crazy."

It's no wonder that so many individuals experience fear and confusion when they tap into their gifts for the first time. As a society we don't arm ourselves with the correct tools, knowledge, or understanding to accept and explore these fascinating skills, nor are we taught these things at school. Add to that countless external forces such as trauma, social media, family expectations, drugs, (both prescription and street), and alcohol, and it's no wonder our gifts are being dulled, muted, and ignored. I could have easily spiraled into fear and disbelief when I had that first experience, assuming that something was seriously wrong with me, or that I was going crazy, because believe me, that first spiritual awakening is anything but sane. When you experience your first awakening, it comes on so strong that you won't even know what hit you. The experience left me feeling like I was on drugs and no longer within my own body. I would describe it almost like a feeling of walking around on a combination of magic mushrooms and ecstasy, except being completely sober and unaware of what was going on, with no one to guide me through it. It was like experiencing the ultimate connectedness but not knowing what to do with it.

All the colors around me were extra vibrant, and the air felt thick. I swear, I could feel every single air particle as it entered and exited my body. Now, as a well mastered psychic, I have these experiences regularly as well as walking others through them, except I now understand and know how to manage, describe, and use them for unique healings on myself and others. One piece of advice I have for anyone who's going through their own spiritual awakening, whether it's their first or their tenth (because you'll have many), is that not everyone will understand and get you. Some will disagree, some will be scared of it, and some will even try to smother it. You'll find out who your real friends are when you're going through any kind of big change. The ones who stick around and support you even though they don't necessarily understand what's happening, are your ride or dies. We don't need to have the same beliefs as everyone else around us and it's not your job to convince anyone of anything. If any "friend" or family member is constantly challenging you on how you decide to live, I would strongly recommend you re-assess the relationship and stop sharing certain things with them. Sometimes you just need to know your audience and pick and choose who to tell what. I don't try to have work convos with people who don't understand my work and I certainly don't ask people for their opinion if they haven't the slightest clue what the fuck I'm talking about. Everyone is on their own path, learning whatever they need to learn for the next step of their own evolution.

When I first started receiving messages, also known as "downloads," it was through a series of images, and pictures, like a slideshow in my head, but I knew they were different from my own ideas, memories, or thoughts. I could tell that they were being delivered through me but not FROM me. I also knew that these messages were meant to be shared with specific individuals. It was then that I realized I was basically like a prophet, which I now call a "channel," the only problem was that I didn't know what the images I was seeing meant.

Think of it like seeing clips of a movie, without knowing what the movie is about. I didn't yet realize that God was showing me symbols that represented something else, to someone else, but he was communicating them to me, in a way that I would understand. In the beginning, I took what I was seeing very literally. This meant that the messages I was delivering often came off like clunky gibberish that made a little bit of sense to some, and absolutely NO sense to others. It was like I was speaking in morse code, but only some people knew how to crack that code. I'm still shocked when I look back, that most of the people I delivered my coded messages to, were actually able to figure them out, and always completely mind blown. It just goes to show you that my gifts were real and what is truly meant to be delivered, will be, no matter how weird and wacky it sounds. These downloads have a purpose even if that purpose isn't crystal clear when I first receive it. At the time, I was delivering these messages (often through text or email) in what I was calling a first draft. Then, the recipient and I would talk back and forth about what each metaphoric sentence meant for them, and together we would assemble all the pieces into sentences and messages that made sense to and for them. With time and practice, I've learned how to communicate my messages with much more ease, and without having to crack codes or trying to put hundreds of pieces together to form a picture. Now, I can easily and immediately translate the visions and movies in my mind, into very precise psychic readings where no first drafts are necessary, and the conversion is instant. It's the same idea as when someone is learning English for the first time. They start with spelling tests, reading, and writing exercises, simple conversations, and build their fluency from there. Eventually speaking, reading, and writing English becomes second nature to them, but it's still going to be an ever growing and evolving process. Think about how long it takes a child to write, spell, and read fluently without mistakes or hesitancy. Even now, we can't nail it all 100% of the time.

Grown adults still make spelling errors and grammar mistakes, but even when it's not perfect, the messages they're communicating can still be received. The same holds true for our psychic mastery levels and expertise. I like to think of tarot cards and angel cards like flash cards. Their purpose is to help us grow and learn. Many people, depending on how their unique intuition works, will add in other tools like plant medicine and crystals to help enhance and guide their gifts.

I work best when I'm able to combine my unique style of coaching with my psychic downloads and visions, dancing between the two, almost like I'm speaking two languages at once. Spanglish anyone? Over time (and I do mean over a full decade) I started to develop a clearer understanding of what each vision meant, and I gathered a library of signature symbols in my mind. These are the symbols that have continued to come up during countless readings for various people from all walks of life. By cataloging these symbols, I've invented my own alphabet, a language which also allows me to deliver messages without delay or hesitation. It's kind of like having Netflix on demand. Now, when I see the symbol of an hourglass for example, I know that it's a sign that my client needs to heal her relationship with time. When I see a ton of black, sticky, and tar like energy, I know that my client is under an extreme amount of pressure and exhaustion, using dark shadow energies like fear and anger to drive them forward. The point here, is that spirit will talk to you in a way that will resonate with you by using feelings and images that you can relate to, understand, and decipher.

Despite the fact that I've done countless nude photoshoots, can talk for hours with strangers about sex, and have the best stories about blow jobs, fuck boys, drunk tanks, and hookups, at my core I'm embarrassingly wholesome. While finalizing this book I asked my husband if he agrees with my statement, about being wholesome, to which he responded, *"you're far from wholesome."* HA - Men! I don't smoke (anymore), and I usually drink alcohol no more than once a year or on super special occasions. However, when I do have that drink, I typically only have one 'level.' Girls gone wild! But, for the most part, I spend my time at home with my boys. I'm in bed by 8 pm watching reality TV, straddling my husband while he tries to focus on the hockey game, and quizzing him to recall specific outfit details and various feelings about our monumental relationship moments. My all-time favorite game to play though is to ask him questions about our relationship. Some of my favorite questions to ask are things like; *What was I wearing the first time you laid eyes on me? When was the exact moment you knew you loved me? If someone broke into our house, would you let them kidnap me in exchange for 5 billion dollars? When did you know for sure that you wanted to claim me as yours, plant your man seed inside of me, and knock me up?* This game never gets old, I'm telling you. I continue to pry out as many details as I can, until he ultimately ignores me, and refuses to continue playing. I went through a phase where I recorded all these little interviews and created a series called *"Richard Reacts"* which was a huge and hilarious hit. At least I thought so.

My happy place is anywhere I can take pictures and videos, capturing moments and memories with my boys; at the lake, riding quads, working out, and motorboating with my husband. That's where the self-made supermodel part of me comes in. I love photoshoots. Booking them, planning them, and posing for them. Whether it's a shoot for my business or brand, with my family, or just a place for me to wear something over the top, I love everything about them. If we're being honest, my biggest motivation for writing this book has been planning what outfit I'll wear for the cover, and book launch party! My family thinks I'm crazy because I'm constantly putting on live, in the flesh, fashion shows at home. Strutting back and forth in the living room to show off whatever new outfit was delivered that week until my husband notices me, gives me a compliment, or suggests we take the fashion show somewhere more private. When this happens (trust me, it happens often) I try to run away as fast as I can before he tackles me onto the bed, attempting to predictably grope, finger, or tickle me. What can I say, he's so easy to thirst trap, and I love him for it.

My motto in life is that I'll always be remembered, whether you hate me or love me, you will never forget me. When I was younger, I ensured this by leading with my more outrageous, wild, and ratchet side. And, while I still love a real good ratchet moment, I am now more confident in leading with my softer, more feminine, healing side when I feel like it. Something I wouldn't have done in my 20's. Now I trust my energy and intuition to present myself in whatever mood I happen to be in at the time. This allows me to create traction and genuine connection with people so that they're able to fully understand who I am, and what they can expect from me, as well as recognize that I'm not some one-dimensional, cookie-cutter, vanilla waffle cone, no opinion, yes woman, boring bitch who apologizes for breathing. People know that I'm loud, proud, funny, and vulgar as well as being incredibly talented, hot, smart AF, and amazing at what I do. I have the confidence to say that at some point, I will likely blow your damn mind. I am not above calling someone a twat bitch, and I'm certainly not sorry about it because my brand is not about being the nice girl in town. I'm someone who loves to be loved but also is ok with being polarizing, poking, and shocking people with my occasional nudity and brash honesty. I'm someone who both catches and holds attention. I'm a truth-teller who was put on Earth to disrupt and occasionally fuck shit up and to tell you the truth, most times, life just isn't that serious. I'm passionate about helping others to heal their past trauma around men, sex, love, health, and money, calling upon my feminine healing energy to be as gentle and caring as someone needs when the time and situation require that softer side. I can do all of this because I alter my punches depending on the severity of the situation. I know when someone needs a tough loving, gentle truth bomb as well as when they need tender loving care. I adapt my channel to my clients and am able to deliver their unique message with the perfect amount of potency.

In the past, when I was younger, I led only with my thirst-trapping self, showing off my body, but always keeping the softer more vulnerable pieces of myself hidden away, safe from being hurt or challenged. And it worked, like a charm I may add. Every time I found myself on the verge of an uplevel, I would channel my "edge factor" which would come out through anger and revenge. Revenge on all the people who discounted my skills, the men who didn't call me back, and the girls who shit-talked behind my back. My goal was to rub my success in their faces, which at the time was my banging revenge body. And, if I'm being completely honest (which I always am), it was incredibly satisfying and still is! But lashing out was the only way I really knew how to move through something. I would get mad, or get even, in order to leave behind the old thing that was pissing me off and step into the new thing that had captured my attention and curiosity. I basically built my entire body and empire on a foundation of a huge "fuck you" and it felt so incredibly good! Try to tell me I can't do something or criticize it and I'll do it ten times harder, then make a point to throw that shit in your face with a special delivery on top. The only downside to this was that I needed to constantly experience anger in my life in order to break through things because when we find a certain way to succeed our bodies and souls remember that path and create a pattern so we can easily repeat it, continuing to have even more success in a way that we already know works. Luckily, I eventually found another way of accomplishing the same thing, without needing anger management classes or starting an Only Fans (*no judgment if you have - seriously - props to you babe - still debating it myself*).

When I was younger, when I was first experimenting with the power of thirst trapping, my hair was limp and thin because of my shitty diet, and constant attempts to lighten my naturally dark locks to Pamela Anderson platinum blonde. All I wanted, and I wanted it badly, was to be hot. I paid insane amounts of money to purchase the perfect pair of jeans that I thought would magically make me look 20 pounds lighter. I spent at least 2 hours getting ready for the bar, coating my face in make-up that was always two shades too light, in an attempt to hide my naturally olive skin. My favorite "hoe trick" was to heat up my black eyeliner with the hairdryer until it was super soft and melted, then apply it to the waterline of my eyes. It gave me the ultimate jet black I was looking for. During this phase of life, I always knew how to work what I had, even at the size I was, knowing that I was far from perfect. I overcompensated by over-sexualizing my body because what I really wanted was to be thinner, to be loved, and to be sought after. I was accessing admiration in the only ways I knew how and the ways I felt I could. Sadly, those ways involved twerking, a large amount of padded cleavage, and a bunch of free hand jobs. Not that those things are bad, and to be honest, they were fun on occasion, but when it meant spiritually bypassing what I really wanted, deep down, these habits weren't serving me. Looking back now, I recognize that the weekends filled with Smirnoff Ice and 3 am Denny's burgers were a real hoot and hollering kind of time in the moment, but they weren't helping my self-esteem issues. I was so clueless, which in a way was kind of nice because I was blissfully eating and drinking without any guilt. At the time, I had no idea about the countless simple changes I could make to trim down my body to where it wanted and was meant to be. Those few skills would have completely changed my choices in men and in life as a whole.

Now, a decade or so later, I'm the vision of stamina and success. My body is perfectly toned in the way I want and although it may fluctuate here and there, just like everyone else, those fluctuations are minor and I still feel decent in my bikini, even on the worst day of my PMS. My idea of a perfect body nowadays is less about being the skinniest girl at the pool, and more about being easily maintainable, looking like a snack, and being able to eat snacks too. My wardrobe choices both then and now, reflect what I'm feeling in my body, owning it, and flaunting it. For the most part, I like to stand out and I enjoy the thought and feeling of all eyes being on me. I've manifested my hair to be thick, long, and luscious, a result of the way I've balanced my nutrition. Now, my body is an easy and effortless representation of my own dreams. When I started combining my food groups together and eating frequently, my hair doubled in thickness and grew twice as fast. Our hair is made of protein. If we think of our bodies as the stem of a flower, that means our hair is the petals and leaves. Just like any kind of plant, our body and hair need the right environment to grow and thrive, and it's our job to make that happen.

You may be thinking, *"Sure Tasha, but it can't really be that easy."* But it is! My top tip for having epic, supermodel hair is to start treating your hair and your body like a cherished garden. One that you want to grow and nurture. Make sure you're connected to your roots, drinking lots of water, getting fresh air, and cultivating a solid foundation made up of good, nutrient-rich food and soil. Otherwise, there's no amount of sunshine or Olaplex that can help you. Minimize the number of extensions, coloring and bleaching you're putting your hair through, as well as the number of times you blast it with heat, either through a hairdryer, flat iron, curling iron, or mermaid barrel. Personally, I let my hair air dry any time I'm not going on camera, and I haven't dyed it in over 9 years, however I'm not sure what my plan will be when I start to eventually grow grey. So far, my plan is just a prayer which goes as follows "*Dear Angels, please keep the pigment in my hair forever while also continuing to help my body thrive. Amen.*" I prayed every day for the angels to help me get through pregnancy without any stretch marks and that worked, so I'm hoping this works too. Right now, I have more white pubes then I do hairs on my head and I'm not that mad about it. I also break all of the "commonly accepted" hair rules by washing mine every single day. I just can't do the whole dry shampoo, dirty hair thing, especially when I work out every day. I use a clarifying shampoo twice a week and switch up my products often, as I believe our hair eventually adapts and needs new things in order to keep thriving. To keep as much volume as possible, I avoid placing any conditioner on my roots and I treat myself to a deep conditioner a few times each week. My message here is that we have to get to the root of everything by managing stress, eating properly, getting enough sleep and also using tools to make it look pretty on the outside. Now, I love makeup, fashion, blowouts, Botox, and even plastic surgery (I've had a couple myself and we'll talk more about that later) but we need to be aware of where we're overcompensating. And, when I do make the decision to have elective surgery, I choose to do it because I'm vain, not because I'm insecure.

Here's the thing, many people are running around, living life, doing questionable things to their bodies, and letting various dicks into their holes. They're under eating, overeating, and getting procedures done without ever actually asking their body and soul what *they* think about the decision. Instead, we need to think about our bodies the same as someone we're in a relationship and partnership with. When we start respecting and treating our bodies the way we want people to treat us, that relationship gets stronger and healthier. The best way to start this practice is to simply ask your body questions. For example, instead of telling your body what it's not allowed to eat, ask what it actually WANTS to eat. Instead of telling your body that it has to complete 100 pushups this morning, ask what it actually WANTS to do to stretch and move.

Before you go and put somebody's dick in your mouth, have you ever thought to ask your mouth how it feels about the situation? Have you ever asked your puss who it wants to fuck or not fuck? Have you ever actually interviewed your butthole to see if it wants to be licked or penetrated? Because you should! Otherwise, this whole thing is just a one-way street and healthy relationships work both ways. Your body is something you should be in constant communication with. And remember, your body can talk to you in all sorts of ways, it's your job to start those conversations though and ask the right questions. Now, the most important part of this whole exercise is that once you've asked your body a question, you have to actually listen for an answer, don't be a rude bitch and just wait for two seconds before you give up. If we've spent a lifetime passive aggressively shit talking and ignoring our bodies, they may not answer right away. If you aren't receiving a response, you may need to ask again, or rephrase the question. It's also important to remember that your mind and soul have a say as well. The goal is to get our body, mind, and soul all on the same page. We can do this by asking all 3 parts of ourselves these same questions and listening for their responses. Now, be prepared because there will be times where all three pieces of yourself don't agree, and conflict arises. For example, let's say that you've asked your body, mind, and spirit, *"What do you think about banging that fuck boy over there?"* Your body may respond with a *"hell yes,"* while your mind says, *"No way bitch, we know how that story goes."*

When our body responds to a man in a certain way, where he makes our crotch tingle, it's likely because of a certain chemistry or craving we're experiencing. And let me tell you, just because you have chemistry or a craving for someone, it doesn't always mean it's a good choice. There's such a thing as toxic chemistry and toxic love. Our body's chemistry can change depending on a lot of different environmental factors that we're responding to. Like our menstrual and ovulation cycle, our stress levels, and our personal triggers and traumas. Our body has a memory of its own and knows when something familiar is also something safe. Which means our body remembers the people, things, and substances that we've used as a means of "healing" in the past. For example, say you're feeling lonely or stressed, you get home, eat ice cream, drink wine, call an ex, or all of the above in no particular order. Your body has now created a catalog of knowledge so that you can store this method of soothing and healing in your very own medicine cabinet for later use. Then, anytime you experience that same familiar emotion your body will remember that the solution is to eat ice cream, drink wine, and call the ex. This is how emotional eating and fuck boy patterns are formed, which in reality are just ways for us to attempt to work through situations while filtering out any discomfort, stress, or pain.

We're literally training our bodies for the marathon of life, which can be a positive and a negative thing. We create so many memories with food and alcohol that even celebrations and family traditions are connected to them, which brings us to comfort eating. If your mom used to cook a lot of hearty and carby casseroles, you'll automatically crave those when you're feeling lost and off track. You'll find yourself eating in an attempt to "come back home" or feel a sense of being nurtured.

One of the best ways to uncover the root cause of why we are the way we are, is to think about one of your typical self-sabotaging behaviors, because we're all either an over doer, an under doer, or a combo of the two which means we avoid one area of life, because we're over-doing things in another area. Whether it be binge eating, binge drinking, numbing out, procrastinating, never completing projects, restricting your diet, over working, over giving, over sucking, or over fucking, we all have our kryptonite.

My point is that we need to inquire with our bodies, minds, and souls when making decisions. Our bodies make decisions based on our past memories. They revert back to old patterns because of a desire for safety and can trick us into repeating self-sabotaging behaviors over and over again. For example, your body may tell you that you have amazing chemistry with a man, but in reality, your body is simply responding to his "edge" factor, recognizing that you'll experience pain while enduring a quick romp session. You're not attracted to him, you're attracted to the idea of him, and the risk of the potential pain he may cause you along with little bits of pleasure or satisfaction you may get by finally changing him and becoming THE one he chooses. Yes, our bodies can get turned on and attracted to pain and emotional punishment, because that's what they're used to. While they crave the intensity and excitement of an unknown thrill, our bodies confuse those feelings with passion and love. You may think you've got great chemistry with a guy who you know is bad for you, but it's actually just your body anticipating a good pounding along with a good heart break and getting off on it. This especially happens for people who numb, avoid, or procrastinate on things. All of the numbing we experience with mindlessly watching tv, over-working, over-eating, over-drinking and over-scrolling makes it so that we need more and more intensity in order to actually feel something. Which leads to our purposely putting ourselves in toxic, often dangerous, situations in order to feel something. Of course, the more this happens, the more toxic these situations have to become.

For example, the more you've been numbing yourself when it comes to your intimate relationships or sexuality, the more you need things to be amped up in the bedroom (or wherever else you're getting it on). This is where violence during sex, and angry fucking come in. And that isn't limited to when you're getting off with a partner. Have you ever used your vibrator so much, or rubbed your bean so roughly, that your orgasms take much longer to come, and lose their potency?

Think of it this way. It's normal and natural to have space and breaks in between our orgasms. The same holds true for our life highs and lows. Life isn't one big walking orgasmic high (darn it right?!). It has both peaks and come downs. And when we don't allow ourselves to be in the come down, to experience our life in neutral, that's when we overcompensate with too much sex, porn, shopping, food, alcohol, work, etc. These are all simply tools and methods we use to create more stimulation in our lives, pushing us back towards the high of thrill chasing. We have to be willing and able to sit alone with ourselves sometimes. No matter how boring we may think it is. And we get to go back to asking our body questions, specific questions, before taking action. If your body says it's turned on by that guy across the bar, ask it why, and request that it show you some other potential options. You can also just explore and keep exploring for as long as you see necessary. If your body is asking for salty chips, again, ask it why. Is it for a practical reason, or an emotional one? It may be that you're tired and your body is desiring carbs to convert into energy so you're able to get through the afternoon, you may be dehydrated and needing the salt from the chips, or you may be craving an emotional impact, which your body believes will be provided by the crunch of chips as your teeth chomp down.

young & innocent

My own struggle with body image, healthy eating, and over-indulging in men all started in grade 10. Looking back now, I can pinpoint the exact moment it happened. A boy that I was crushing on told me "*Those pants make your legs look fat*," and just like that, his observation was etched into my memory bank and became a part of my life story, and identity. Not to mention starting what would be a lifetime mission to find the perfect pair of pants that would make my legs look skinny. I was wearing a pair of really bomb (at the time) super wide-leg jean overalls, sitting awkwardly on a bench with my legs pressed down against the seat. This boy simply spoke aloud the insecurities I was already thinking and had playing through my mind, because our thoughts create our reality. Now, many years later, I find that men and people in general have a habit of doing this. They voice, out loud, our worst insecurities, and most of the time they say it in a very matter of fact kind of way. I've come to realize that this is actually an attempt from our souls to neutralize the shame we feel, by pulling it out of our subconscious for us to look at and address.

I'm sure that boy probably had zero clue what he'd said, or the effect it had on me. In fact, he said it in a quite nonchalant and matter of fact way. He wasn't actually trying to be mean or hurt my feelings, he was just expressing something he noticed. None of us were all that self-aware back then. But his simple offhanded comment combined with a ton of other shit affected my intimacy with men and clients for years to come. A funny sidenote, later that year I got my sweet revenge on him. I had a real good buzz going, well, if we're being honest, it was more than a buzz, I was probably closer to being wasted, and I enticed that same boy away from a party with the promise of a blow job or the insinuation at least. Who knows exactly what I said to snag his attention, something super thirst trappy and straight forward would have been on brand for me back then. I pulled that boy by the hand beside this house and then into the back seat of a car. We made out a little. I yanked his pants down, around his ankles, and then very promptly and swiftly turned around and left him sitting there. In his shitty, ripped seat, partially rusted Toyota. Half-naked. With blue balls and a pointless boner. (I'd actually forgotten all about this situation until writing this book and cannot stop laughing! I swear, everyone needs to write a book, it'll heal you in ways you could never have imagined.)

My actions that night were intentional and very strategically planned. What can I say, Karma's a bitch. That wasn't the only boy I did this to either. It went on to become a classic move of mine, which in hindsight was a seriously dangerous game to play. I realize now as a grown woman the big problems I could have caused myself by fucking with guys like that. I played out this same scene countless times, in various settings, anywhere from a pit party bush to a friend's house, and hidden boot rooms at house parties. I had no clue I was doing it, but with my little cock tease moves, I was healing myself and taking my power back. I do have to say that although it was highly immature and like I said, actually very dangerous and not a good idea at all, I do NOT regret doing this, specifically with one guy in particular that I actually liked and was crushing on quite hard. I pulled my same old classic stunt with him, and then found out after the fact that he and one of his bros had a bet going for who could hook up with me first. Finding out that I was something to be bet upon made me feel completely worthless, embarrassed, and small. But here's the thing, I was playing games with boys, which in turn meant that I was attracting boys who would play games with me. Write that shit down. When you play games with boys trying to tease them or make them chase you, all you get is boys who want to play the game back and lose interest after the chase is over.

Even after delivering my little doses of sweet revenge, the accumulation of various comments throughout my life, from "*you used to be hot*" to "*you're so cute*," and "*your legs look fat in those pants*," caused me to erect a protective and emotional forcefield around myself, which quickly developed into an actual physical forcefield of extra fat on my body, weight gain, and purple stretch marks on my hips and thighs. I had no idea at the time that by hiding my true personality or relying on alcohol for the courage to let it come out, I was stopping myself from forming genuine connections or experiencing what I really wanted, which was a husband or long-term boyfriend. The only way I knew how to be close to a man was through physical touch, which was much easier than pushing past my shyness and allowing myself to be treated the way I truly wanted to be. The more those cute girl comments stuck with me, the shyer I became, and the lower my standards dropped until I started using alcohol as a crutch and a confidence booster to break through my shyness and turn into the wild girl and life of the party. A girl who didn't give a fuck and would say and do anything for the shock factor and a reaction. I used my drunkenness as a way to be who I really wanted to be, which was someone who gets whatever she wants without hesitation. I would walk around the bar feeling like I was in my own slow motion music video where everyone either wanted to fuck me or be me. Having a buzz on made me truly feel like I was an unstoppable smoke show in my mini bodycon dresses, fake lashes (sometimes even 2 sets doubled up), and knee-high boots.

My method of quickly getting a man's attention was always through working what I knew I had, and I kept his attention by impressing him with hand jobs, reverse cowgirls, and bj's that came along with very exaggerated cum slurping sounds (forehead slap). I was the ultimate performer, and I took pride in how I could easily put on a one-woman porn star show. My greatest confidence came from my biggest insecurity, of not being good enough, not being loved. The hotter the guy, or the bigger the challenge, the more value I would assign myself. For example, even when I was at my heaviest, I always loved showing my body off with mini dresses, hooker boots, and the fast pace in which I can shake my tush. I was pretty confident that I could effectively and efficiently thirst trap almost any guy with my tits and ass, but at the same time, I desperately wished

I were thinner. My body was both my biggest strength and biggest weakness at the same time. *Spoiler: If we lead with our body, sexuality, and hotness, it shouldn't be a shocker that we attract men whose top priority is getting to that body and sexuality.* I started to notice that I had a pattern. I attracted hot guys who worshiped my body and praised me for the night, or many nights, that we spent together. But they would never actually commit to a relationship. Or I would attract average looking guys who treated me like gold but held zero attraction for me. The problem was never getting the guy, the problem was always getting the right guy, and getting them to stick around. The hot ones that I actually wanted, hid me in their basements like some sort of secret, and the average ones took me out on dates only to bore, underwhelm, and disgust me to death.

While I'm still a proud thirst trapper, I own and love everything that I've done to get to where I am today, including the things that make me laugh and cringe all at the same time, although I do thank God that all we had were crappy flip phones back then (less photographic evidence). My thirst trap looks a little different now. After years of ego deaths, mind fucks, and intense sexual awakenings, I'm able to merge my thirst-trapping side with the more intimate and soft parts of who I am. I call this my wholesome good girl and my ratchet bad girl coming together to hang out and join forces. It's the relationship of my sweet and my salty. Once I've gotten your attention with my banging body, glam of the day, and tantric dance moves. Once you've picked your jaw back up off the floor, and your eyes are back on mine, I'm going to help you to heal yourself, from the inside out. I lead with both my heart and my body, working together as a team and I see them both as having equal value in my life, my work, and my relationships.

Each of us possess 2 different sides, or personalities if you will. The good girl, and the bad girl. Only once we've done a fair amount of healing work can we begin to see, balance, and recognize both sides of ourselves, without allowing one or the other to take over the show. It's all about collaboration between the two and knowing which is best suited for each situation we experience. Our bad girl side usually makes an appearance when someone is trying to fuck us around. She's there to remind us of our backbone and make sure that no one, and I mean no one, takes advantage of us. She can be edgy and hasty, but without her, we can easily become a doormat. Our good girl side is grace and understanding. She knows how to forgive and accept people and is very aware and sensitive of other's feelings. Without her, we can easily become a miserable and angry bitch, but we sometimes have to remind her that not every person will see, respect, or deserve the best we have to offer because otherwise she goes into unnecessary ball licking and people pleasing. Put your hand up if you've ever sucked a hairy, unmanicured nutsack. Because we all know you didn't actually WANT to do that. This is why it's so important that we embrace both sides of ourselves. To recognize when we're being guided to firm the fuck up, suck less hairy nutsacks and take a stand, or when we're being guided to soften our blows, give a little more and show some compassion. My clients describe working with me and my gifts, like receiving a sisterly hug, a loving bitch slap, and a soothing bath which may potentially lead to steamy sex all at once. It's intimacy, friendship, laughter, and healing all combined into the perfect potion.

Each and every one of us have our own experiences and traumas that we carry throughout our daily lives, whether it be from our relationships with men or other women, personally or professionally. And, we have the choice of disrupting those patterns and implementing change in whatever ways we see fit. We can do this like the good girl, nice and gentle with ease and tender care, or we can do it like the bad girl, potently with the power of a wrecking ball that chews you up and spits you out. Neither one is truly right or wrong, sometimes a gentle touch isn't enough, and other times passionate aggression only serves to stoke the fire. So, if you're a fiery wrecking ball, own it, and don't be sorry for who you are. If you're a delicate fairy, own it, and don't allow others to influence you. Remember, your unique ways of living and existing are your gifts, and we can each command and control our gifts just like a magical potion. Made up from the recipe of what we desire for our lives. When we find others that we look up to. Maybe it's a friend, a mentor, or public figure who possesses qualities that you admire. These things can be taught, learned, and added to your recipe as often as you desire. What matters is that the recipe you create is uniquely yours and cannot be fucked with or tainted by anyone else.

SPIRITUAL HOTNESS CHALLENGE

ROCK CHALLENGE

Collect a few large rocks as well as some basic paints & sharpies. Spend a few moments asking your soul what it is that you desire more. Then, using that energy, paint or doodle an image on one of your rocks. Turning your thoughts and desires into tangible results that you can see, touch & hold. Now, plant your rock Somewhere you feel powerful, balanced, and at peace. This may be a local park, a beach, a mountainside, etc. By planting your rocks in a public place you're not only sending your spell into the world but also spreading your soul's magic without your ego's desire for recognition. For example; if you'd like to call in true love, you may choose to paint/draw a key & a heart, including a quote or phrase on the back of the rock. Or, if you'd like for your partner to communicate with you more, you may choose to paint/draw an envelope with a heart. Some of my rocks have included spells for scaling my business, with a doodle of a rocket ship, a Palm tree symbolizing the trips I desire to take with my family, a camera, a bikini, and a cupcake because I desire to continue loving my body, posing for photoshoots & enjoying sweets whenever I choose to.

SPIRITUAL
HOTNESS CHALLENGE

ATTRACTION CHALLENGE

Picture someone you're attracted to and start to think about them. As you're thinking about them, bring your attention to your body. What body part stands out the most while thinking of them? What does that body part represent to you and how does it relate to that person? What emotions arise? What chakra does it land closest to and what elements does that chakra represent? For example, when I think about richard, I feel it in my puss which is also my root chakra. The root chakra represents grounding, support and safety. However, if I am feeling angry at him, my body may respond differently. You can play around and picture various people in your life who you like or dislike, and see how your body responds with the thought of them and why.

CHAPTER 1

BE A BITCH FASTER

"I'm willing to let people get mad at me, if it means that I never have to get mad at myself for holding back who I am. No matter how holy you are, you'll always be somebody's villain"

Growing up I was so shy that I was basically a borderline mute. I only spoke when I had to, and talking to boys was out of the question. They genuinely scared me. If I'm being totally honest, not much has really changed there, and to this day I've still never had a really close male friend. Unless it's a client. I still get shy having anything more than a surface-level conversation with any man other than my husband. We lived in the country, away from the excitement of the city, our TV had only 2 channels with the most risqué shows available being *Ricki Lake* and *Unsolved Mysteries* and our biggest adventure was riding a bike to the store for freezies and candy. When I talk to girls who have lived in big cities, usually their lives were completely different than my own. While I was still innocently getting excited about penny candy, they were sneaking out, meeting up with boys and pushing edges I had not yet discovered. I was definitely a late bloomer as far as scandal and rule-breaking goes. I also was the last one to get my period. I distinctly remember the first time I learned to put a tampon in, fighting with one of those awful cardboard installers, at a friend's house while they all pep-talked and cheered me on through the door during our lunch hour. I had put off using tampons for so long because I was scared they would make my vagina loose, but eventually I knew it was time to take the plunge and shove that thing up my hole. Before then, I'd never explored myself down there. I'd never looked at it with a mirror, touched it, rubbed my clit, or anything else. I didn't have my first orgasm until I was 17 when my friends bought me a pink see-through vibrator. Despite my shyness, I did have an amazing group of girlfriends who helped encourage me to get curious, and they still remain my besties to this day.

When I was 17, I flipped through an issue of Cosmo and saw an article about hummers, head, fellatio. The headline said something like, *"The Top 3 Tips to Provide a Memorable Experience."* For whatever reason, the article stuck with me, and I ended up giving my first BJ just a few weeks later at a bonfire party with friends where I also happened to get drunk for the very first time. I remember sort of sneakily planning everything out in my mind, starting with which guys I would talk to once I was drunk. It almost felt like alcohol was my free pass to do and be whatever I wanted. So, I proceeded to chug a 2 liter of Boone's Farms, and when I say chug, I really mean chug. I was scared that somehow, I wouldn't get drunk enough to follow through with my plan, and I figured the best way to ensure inebriation was to drink as much as I could, as fast as I could, and for as long as I could. Sweet Jesus, that was a horrible choice, and a pattern that I repeated for nearly 3 years before I realized there were other ways of getting and staying drunk. Anyhow, once I was good and juiced up, I stumbled my way across the party to choose my target. I took his hand and we snuck away from the group to hide in this weird junkyard where I proceeded to get down on my knees, pop his wiener in my mouth, and give it a real good and thorough hum. And, when I say hum, I mean it. That was all I did. There was no head bobbing or swirling tongue action going on. I kept his peen in my mouth with zero movement. Seriously, if you're picturing someone blowing on a kazoo, that's exactly what happened. I hummed until I ran out of air, refilled my lungs, and hummed some more. I can't tell you how many times I restarted my humming until eventually, he was like, *"okay, that's good."* Clearly, the poor guy was bored to death and probably also just as confused as I was and grasping at straws to find a polite way of asking me to stop.

I should have stopped. Any normal human being would have stopped at that point, but no, not me. I'm not a quitter. While he was definitely over the experience, I felt like there had to be something more profound at the end of a successful BJ. Keep in mind that 16-year-old me, had no idea what cum or orgasms actually were. So, I just kept going, humming, breathing, and humming some more with his teenage wiener sitting stagnantly in one spot on my tongue. You'd think that I would find this memory cringy, but I don't. It's one of my most glorious stories and absolutely hilarious no matter how you look at it. I've often wondered if that boy ever thinks back to that one time a girl hummed on his dick for half an hour after he politely requested that she stop, twice. I'm telling you, I make impacting and life-lasting memories with people, and I've been remembered since 1999. Even if it's not in the way I prefer. Looking back on it now as an adult, I am happy that I stayed innocent as long as I did, and it would have been more concerning to me if I knew how to give an epic BJ at 16 years old.

Ever since I was a little girl, I've dreamt of being a model. Not just any model, a supermodel. When I was 13, I went to my first scouting event, hoping, and praying that I'd be discovered and chosen to model for a magazine or commercial. Of course, I was never chosen, but I had friends who were. I went on to attend numerous events, but I was never tall enough, had bad teeth, was too quiet and shy, and never what they wanted. I would go home devastated and cry for days, feeling like I was never going to be good enough. Never talking to my mom about anything I was feeling, which looking back now would have changed a lot of things in the following years. If only I'd had the skills or prompts to communicate with an adult about those feelings.

My parents never asked a lot of questions. Not because they didn't care, they were just busy with their own lives, working, raising a family, and doing the best they could. My mom had her own way of making me feel better. She would take pictures of me, and my friends and I think that was her way of helping me feel like a model. There were hugs, but never conversations about self-esteem, self-worth, beauty, or why I hadn't been chosen. So, I just figured it out on my own through trial and error. My friends have always been my pillars of support and they were always there to pick me up in the best ways a 13-year-old knows how.

In my mind, I was never going to be what other people thought of as pretty. As a dark-haired, olive-skinned Chinese German, I didn't fit the stereotype of what a model should look like back then. Magazines were filled with pictures of Pamela Anderson, Kate Moss, and Claudia Schiffer. It was the era of tall, skinny, blonde bombshells. Throughout school there was only ever one other Chinese girl, so I knew I was at least a little different, but at the same time I was unaware of my feelings and emotions and what that even meant. In 8th grade, I started box-dying my naturally very dark hair, attempting to bleach it, or using Sun-In in hopes of achieving my desired Pamela Anderson Blonde. I didn't have the money to visit a salon, so I just tried to wing my way through the process, until my entire head was fried, blonde in spots but mostly orange, and so thin and sparse that it always looked flat and dry. One time I had the worst bad dye job done and I remember trying to attempt fixing the spots by blending them in with eyeshadow which did not work FYI.

striking a pose

Then, something happened. Puberty hit and my body started morphing from a girl into a woman. That's when I first started drinking alcohol and my eating habits began to include more and more fast food and junk food. Because my mom was no longer packing my lunch for school I blissfully ate McDonald's fries and chicken sauce every day with my friends, never really thinking about what it could and would do to my weight. I also got my first job, waitressing at a Chinese restaurant, and part of my pay was being able to eat for free. So, I would often eat deep-fried wontons, sweet and sour pork, and fried rice at the buffet 4-5 days a week and as you would guess, I started packing on the pounds.

Once I started junior high school, one of the girls decided that being popular was more important than being nice, so she started some lame backstabbing rumor about a boy. Honestly, I can't even remember what the rumor was, just that it definitely wasn't true, and it put a huge target on my back with many of the other kids at school. Especially the most popular, cool, intimidating, older kids, including all of the crushable heartthrob boys in school. All of the girls from that group were older than me and made no secret of the fact that they hated me, with their glares and outright threats. It got to the point where every day I would anticipate going to school and my body would literally start to shake because of how scared I was that I was going to get beat up. Back then, bullying wasn't a concern like it is today. Nobody ever talked about it and there was nothing in place to prevent it. I think it was just assumed that everything was 'kids being kids.'

I never knew if someone was going to creep up behind me and when one of them did run into me in a vacant hallway, they would either insult me or threaten to beat me up. My approach was always to ignore and walk away, but do you know how scary and traumatizing that is for an already shy and mute girl who is literally petrified of boys and meeting new people? Honestly, they chose what they thought was the weakest link because I had done literally nothing but keep my head down and go to class. I lived an entire year in fear, never telling my parents about anything, or communicating what was going on to a single teacher or adult. Finally, I'd had enough of the threats and whispers, and somehow little mute me took a stand. It was a regular day in grade 8 and those same popular older girls were whispering in the same old dumbass way to one another, until one approached me and said, *"So and so wants to fight you,"* but instead of cowering I said, *"Bring It!"* With not a single pep talk from an adult, not a single conversation with anyone else to help guide me through the situation, I somehow knew I had to do something. A big circle of our classmates formed around us; the whole girl gang, and me. We scrapped it out right then and there. There was a lot of hair pulling and arm flailing. I was wearing a little floral printed dress, not the best fight attire, and I was scared, confused, and really, trying to survive. I was also still holding myself back. I had literally done nothing ever, to this girl or any of the other girls cheering her on. Hell, I hadn't even spoken with most of them. I'd never used or experienced physical violence before, so the idea of hitting someone felt completely unnatural. I did the best I could at the time, but I definitely wasn't going full out. I can tell you that the other girl definitely wasn't holding back. She went completely wild and crazy like a demon took over her soul. Looking back, I can see the whole experience now in my mind which actually helps me to understand more about what was happening energetically. I can play back and see the other girl losing herself to a dark, blackout rage, which was actually just triggered by an abandonment wound and her own pressure to be somebody. Nobody attacks anything unless they feel threatened, and she may not have specifically felt threatened by me, but by something else in her own life.

The more someone feels in danger or out of control in their own lives, the more they will seek out ways to feel strong and in power, in whatever ways they can. I was that for her, a way for her to feel powerful and a part of something bigger, by ganging up on me with her crew to egg her on. In the end, I believe the big fight was a draw, with no one winning or losing, although I did walk away with some bites and bruises. I can't help but laugh out loud right now as I write this. For a long time, I didn't realize it, but that one fight was a major dictator in my life, and it actually created a whole new pattern of behavior for me down the road. I remember so badly wishing that I had a big brother or a big sister there to defend me or make me feel safe, and I know now that the lesson I was meant to learn was how to defend and stand up for myself. The fight was a reflection of keeping all of my feelings locked inside, never asking for help and never communicating with my parents or teachers. It forced me to use my voice in a way that was extremely out of character and uncomfortable, in order to make it out alive.

the beginning of my bad girl era

Soon after that fight, the school year ended, and the older kids moved on to high school. Everything seemed to calm down and school was fun to go to again. However, I'd continue to run into those jerks over the next few years at bush parties and bars, with similar scenarios playing out every so often. I remember once, in my early 20s, crossing paths with one of the main girls at a house party. And, while you'd have thought we'd have matured, it was exactly the same scenario as it had been in high school. She sat there, eyeballing me all fucking night, taunting me, wearing her same go-to outfit that hadn't changed in 10 years, until finally I looked straight into her big black pupils and asked, *"What the fuck are you looking at?!"*

Before I knew it, she'd punched me right in the eye. I'm proud to say I got in a few good hits as well, but right there, in the living room of somebody's house, I watched as we played out the same high school pattern of behavior. This time though, I caught onto something smarter. Sporting my fresh new shiner, which I was low-key proud of, I realized that the person who starts the fight, WINS it. Whoever lands the first punch, gets a head start. They have the upper hand, the surprise, and the shock value. The other person needs time to compose themselves for a comeback which is harder to do after a fresh punch in the eyeball. I decided right then and there that I would never be bullied or lose again. Going forward, I would make the first move as a means of self-preservation and regardless of my shiner, I actually felt pretty damned tough. I saw my first black eye as a token of strength, something to be proud of. I didn't know it back then, but that shiner was like a trophy I'd won after years of torment. It showed that I wasn't scared, and it meant that I'd taken my power back, used my voice, and stood up for myself. It stood for something bigger and told the world that I wasn't going to back down. I'm not scared of you or the hatred you have toward yourself, that you project onto me. That was the moment when everything changed, I stopped being the shy, quiet good girl who didn't swear and was afraid of talking to boys, and I became somewhat of the aggressor, looking for a fight. I continued this behavior well into my 20s, using alcohol as liquid courage to pick fights with anyone who looked at me wrong, all in an attempt to make up for that first fight I'd been thrown into out of a pure desire to survive.

Things at home weren't great, the relationship with my parents was tense and I moved out on my own by the time I was in grade 12. I was going to school full-time, working 2 jobs, and eating as

high school graduation

much free food at work as I could to save money for rent and other expenses. I started gaining a lot of weight and as the number on the scale went up, my self-esteem plummeted. The more overweight I became, the more I relied on alcohol to come out of my shell, and the more I leaned into sexual behavior to gain attention and affection.

I drank to get drunk, to lose my inhibitions, and to wake up the confident wild side of myself. I danced on bars, loving the feeling of knowing that all eyes were on me. I cherry-picked which men I wanted, and I was always successful, but the ones I really liked nearly always ended up as sneaky nighttime rendezvous, while the ones who took me out on nice dates lost my interest immediately. Some of my secret flings even lasted as long as 3 years! Have you ever had someone booty call you for 3 years while you basically thought you were deeply and madly in love? *Insert eyeroll.* I used my sexuality to impress, overperforming in bed doing everything I thought I should, to be memorable and to leave an impression, and let me tell you, I highly doubt any of those guys forgot about me.

It wasn't until I met my husband that I realized what I'd been doing. I'd been performing, putting on a show, and with him, he was already impressed by who I was, as an actual human being and woman. He was attracted to my personality and loved me for me, not who I was trying to be. He didn't need me to put on a show, because he was already in awe of me, at my most natural and normal state and we had a real connection. I no longer needed to dance on the bar, or put on a show for strangers, although I do still occasionally give dances at home when the mood strikes. Even today, I love to dress up and put on catwalk shows for him. Walking back and forth in front of him and my kids across the living room, twirling around in various outfits until he has no choice but to pay attention to me. The catwalk show is followed by me asking him to rate his top favorite outfits in order of priority and express in specific detail why he likes each one. We are who we are and even though I don't really drink now, I'm doing the same things I've always done, flaunting myself across the room, but in much healthier atmospheres and without the need to numb myself. I still enjoy the idea of impressing him and having all eyes on me, but I'm doing it from a place of full instead of empty and not giving my goods away without receiving love in return.

The same thing goes for communication in relationships. I can easily have hard conversations with my husband because I know that our love isn't fickle. I don't sit there pussy footing around or passive-aggressively pretending I'm not mad or sad about something. I'm upfront about it immediately without fear of his reaction. I'm able to do this because I know he loves all of the pieces of me, even the ugly ones. We're never afraid to hash things out and we don't sweep things under the rug or let things build up, but we are able to let things go and pick and choose our battles. For me, it's less about trying to avoid an argument, and it's more about learning how to roll through them easier.

When we, as women, hold back the skanky, ghetto, and gnarly pieces of ourselves, they always find a way of leaking out into another area of our lives, no matter what. For example, if you're pissed off about an interaction you've had with someone online, at work, or in your family, but bite your tongue instead of saying what you really want to, you're probably going to find yourself being extra snitty and snarly with your husband or the people closest to you. You may snap at them for something stupid and petty, taking your frustration out on them, instead of that bitch online, or that family member who's always poking at you. It's crazy how we torture the ones who love us the most, instead of actually speaking the truth to the ones who don't. The same holds true if you're feeling some type of way about your husband or partner, not expressing your true thoughts because you're trying not to hurt his feelings and to 'stay positive.' Or perhaps half-ass asking for whatever it is you really want or need because you don't want to feel like a burden. Those things are all going to come through in your career, friendships, and family relationships.

Trust me, take a minute and think about the last week, year, or month. When have you buried your thoughts or feelings about a person or situation, only to blow up on someone or something else completely unrelated to the original issue? Feels pretty shitty right? That's usually followed by a self-imposed guilt trip and beating ourselves up for NOT doing what we really wanted to do, which was finally saying what we meant. Because we squish this all down, mixing it with all of the other crapola in our lives so that when it does come out, it explodes in bigger and more hurtful ways than if we'd said something in the beginning. Our desire to be nice, kind, and be liked literally ends up hurting people more in the end. Ourselves included.

When we hold ourselves back from speaking our peace, we wind up lashing out in other areas, punishing ourselves, and others with our pent-up resentment. I challenge you to think of it this way. Every time something happens, and you make the decision to not speak up, you're eating a piece of poop. Yup, poop. Now, you're going through life, being nice to everyone around you, but they can all smell the poop on your breath. Nothing you do is going to hide the fact that you're eating your own toxic poo sandwich, and if the smell isn't coming out on your breath, it's definitely going to be noticeable in the extra 10 pounds on your pooch. Suddenly holding it all in doesn't seem like such a great idea, does it?

The answer is simple. Be a bitch faster. I use this concept in my marriage, friendships, and professional relationships with clients and colleagues. By saying the things I want to say right away, and owning my thoughts and feelings, I'm able to move past and through things much faster than if I were to obsess over how I should react. People are stronger than we think, and if they're going to hate you for being yourself, and having a moment of bitchy freedom, LET THEM. Let them know who you are right from the start. You don't need to go around insulting people or just being heinous to everyone, but you do need to stop thinking everyone around you is too weak to handle your hotness or whatever it is that you have to say. It's not true, and the reality is that it's not them you're trying to protect, it's yourself. Think about that for a moment. You may think people can't handle the truth of what you have to say, but really, it's you who can't handle saying your own truth. It is possible, to be direct and forward, while still having grace and understanding for people. Also, sometimes grace and understanding will get you nothing but a shit sandwich and you need to draw the line and tell people to get fucked.

This is one of the reasons why it's so important that you be boldly authentic in every setting because when you're not, you'll end up having a bunch of people in your life who expect you to keep being whatever good girl image you're trying to portray, which is easily the most exhausting thing on the planet. Eventually, you will fuck up (everybody does) and when you do, those people you've been trying to protect will be mad that you're not the image of perfection you've made yourself out to be. They'll have invested in the polite, perfectly curated version of you, which leaves you trapped and committed to living a life that isn't yours. The more you focus on pampering people's feelings and tiptoeing around those raw and honest topics, the more they'll come to expect that from you, and you'll be forever sentenced to being the subdued motherly tit they suckle on for comfort.

Let's dig into WHY we do this. A lot of people understand and recognize that they're holding themselves back from being fully authentic, but they don't know how to stop or have given up on even trying. They want to unleash what's brewing within their core and step into their flaming truth, but it feels intimidating, scary, and fucking impossible.

For many of the women I've worked with, this has been a regular issue when it comes to their relationship with their sex lives and men, when they've stopped holding back and fucked someone they shouldn't have. Maybe they had an affair, screwed somebody's boyfriend, or betrayed a friend. They've fully embraced going for something "bad" or "wrong" or done something scandalous and been left with feelings of guilt and shame after the fact. It was a moment when they allowed themselves to be truly carefree and untamed, but there was a negative side effect that came with it. This then drives them to link their passionate actions with seeing their sexuality and hotness as being something bad and rule-breaking, something they should be ashamed of and hide away, yet they are also secretly happy about it because they allowed themselves to be selfish and do what they really wanted to do. This is what I like to call the birth of the bad girl.

Ask yourself, when was the first time you remember breaking the rules? What were the consequences of your actions? What punishment or consequence came with it? Often, when we're experiencing the birth of our inner bad girl, the experience can be toxic. This can also show up in other areas of our lives like with our food and spending habits.

Personally, my inner bad girl, rule breaker showed up as binge eating, drinking excessively, starting bar fights, fucking people's boyfriends, and making a series of questionable *"I don't give a fuck' decisions."* Needless to say, these were not my proudest moments, but the key thing to remember is that we're only doing these things in an attempt to take back our power and seek revenge for the things we feel jolted by. These actions are just our soul's way of evening out the playing field and to be honest, I don't feel guilty, because guilt is just the inability to own that you did what you wanted to do, and I was really just feeling my way into being a better version of myself with various experiences to learn and grow from.

The birth of our bad girl happens for a reason, usually, because we've been raised in a home where we felt powerless in part because of the rules, restrictions, and expectations set for us by our parents, guardians, and ourselves. For example, let's say you have a parent, girlfriend, or partner that constantly makes you feel like you're not pretty or skinny enough. Having numerous boyfriends or men on your roster is one way to assure yourself that you are in fact pretty and skinny enough as proven by your abundance of men. It's a quick way to make up for the loss of love and control that you're missing in another area of your life by having numerous men choose you. Let's look at food for example. Say that as a child you were given a lot of food restrictions, told not to eat certain things, or not to gain weight. Well, a good way to say fuck you to all the rules is to continuously eat everything you were told not to. Again, just to prove that you can. Whether it be extra cookies or extra dicks going into our mouths, it's a way for us to break the rules and do exactly what we were told not to.

Bad decisions are almost always made after a period of withholding from something, whether it be stifling our words, our puss, our carbs, our self-care, or our personality. A lifetime of silencing ourselves only leads to blow-ups and breakups that will be much harder than necessary. By setting out to break the rules, what we're really doing is disrupting our good girl, people-pleasing patterns. So, while the birth of our bad girl may be a period filled with what we initially see as bad decisions, every single action we take is in its own way healing us.

Each and every one of us is meant to come to Earth in order to feel things. But, when we're constantly focused on avoiding those feelings, and instead rely on food, alcohol, work, and men to feel things, more extreme measures are eventually required in order for us to notice when change is needed, for us to truly feel alive. This is what I call an addiction to intensity.

Usually when we have an addiction to intensity, it shows up as an extreme repelled-ness from feelings of boredom or 'meh' normal feelings. I consider this our neutral setting. It's where we actually don't feel bad at all, but we also don't feel overly good. We feel neutral, normal. I spent far too many years running away from feeling anything close to normal because I related it to feeling very average and underwhelming. I didn't want a life of the things that normal people represented, because I thought that meant failure. I thought I needed to always be achieving, ahead of my peers, thriving, and passionately excited, which in actuality is not healthy at all. It's an addiction to goal achievement and go-getting in order to prove to both yourself and other people, that they were wrong about who they thought you were. Success and intensity addiction will often show up as people saying things like, *"I thrive in chaos"* or *"I just get bored really easily,"* as well as when they get extremely irritated by people who are laid back, seeing it as a sign of laziness. An addiction to intensity can make us think and feel like every single minute of every day needs to be spent being productive, throwing ourselves into situations that may be draining and exhausting, all because we believe that any time spent sitting still is a waste. We'd rather feel anything, including hurt, exhaustion, anger, or frustration than stagnancy or boredom. We relate pain and tiredness to growth.

Have you ever thought to yourself, *"I'd rather die than be bored?"* Or found yourself in bed with an ex, or a stranger, because you'd rather have a body beside you then no body at all? What we're doing in these moments is creating a cycle of ego deaths, blowing up our relationships, bodies, businesses, and bank accounts, in order to avoid that dreaded neutral feeling of being bored, and seeking out the intense feelings of anger, passion, frustration, excitement, etc. We've trained our bodies to desire intensity; in whatever form it may take. This may manifest itself by self-sabotaging with food and overeating to the point where you begin putting on weight, which you ignore at first, but once that weight gain reaches the point where your clothes no longer fit, you get angry and commit to joining a gym. Again, ignoring the problem while it's a subtle 3 lbs., until you create an intense anger at yourself, because that's the only time you actually get moving. You crave intensity so desperately that you ignore the nudges and whispers from your body, begging for change. Instead, you wait until it's screaming at you. Because deep down, you unconsciously can't stand to feel content and at peace. You cause chaos in your body and life until you're forced to get your ass to the gym and get moving. Which in turn means spending 10 days in a row, at the gym, working out until you're exhausted and ready to drop or crash dieting before your trip to Mexico.

We find ourselves creating problems, in order to feel happy with ourselves, finding the temporary feelings of pain, exhaustion, or guilt as solutions, as "success." And the cycle continues. The same cycle holds true with money. If you have an addiction to intensity or pressure, you will let your bank accounts deplete fully before taking action to replenish them, because you only feel urgency when you're being driven by fear and hustle. It's the fear of being broke, the fear of being fat, the fear of being a failure, that propels us into action. This is why so many people are only able to successfully lose weight before a big trip, event, or milestone. Because there's something on the line that they're fearful of. They have a set deadline that they're afraid of missing and they are not willing to look or feel fat in a bikini, so they finally take action through pressure.

Other people are the opposite and react to pressure and fear by completely shutting down, never doing anything about it, and avoiding those trips, events, and milestones altogether. These are the good girls. They shrink away from passion while the bad girl moves impulsively towards the fire. Where are you seeing these patterns in your own body, career, and love life? Do you hold back from spending time, money, and attention on yourself, or are you consistently overspending? Do you find yourself overeating or undereating? Do you under-fuck or over-fuck? How do you feel through these cycles? What would it take to break that cycle for you?

Our inner bad girl is a disruptor to help us evoke change. When you feel her stepping in, it's because your inner good girl is fiddle fucking around, and your bad girl has had enough of the bullshit. It's important that we find ways to heal our relationships with both of these women who live within us, having conversations with them, and seeking to understand the why behind their actions. Too often we try to fight these impulses, which only serves to feed them, further sabotaging all areas of our lives.

Many people, women especially, move through life, unaware of the feelings and codes buried deep within them like secrets and uncovered skeletons in the closet. Missing parts of themselves that they never fully realize because they don't yet know where to look. We exist in a world that urges us to filter our thoughts, feelings, and words, sharing only the nice parts of ourselves, locking anything that doesn't fit that picture-perfect, pleasant mold, inside of our bodies like poison. But I've got news for you bitch! That filter of niceness doesn't help anyone. Instead, it allows that poison to fester inside of your body like rotting garbage that builds and builds until you can't contain it anymore, and you eventually blow up. It's literally as if you're eating other people's shit and pretending it's ice cream while at the same time having poo stuck between your teeth. It fools no one! And no matter how nice you are, your breath is still going to smell like shit. There is no amount of spearmint gum that'll cover the stench. That's why I refuse to pussyfoot around the truth in order to prevent hurt feelings. Whether I'm feeling intense or gentle, skanky or kind, I honor my energy and feelings. I honor my inner bitch and refuse to exist behind a filter of pretend niceness.

People will try to tell you to keep your personal and professional lives separate. But as women, it's important that we recognize how closely intertwined all areas of our lives are, and I do mean all areas. Whether we value short or long-term relationships directly relates to how we manage our businesses, our weight fluctuations, our marriage, kids, friendships, co-workers, and clients.

Think of it this way, if you're someone who has a lot of one-night stands or bene-friend relationships, you're more likely to experience blocks and resentment around the idea of short-term career moves. Because those relationships and connections feel unsafe for you. They make you feel used and undervalued like you've been taken from or have given away more than you've received in the form of time, effort, thoughts, and orgasms. Or it may be the opposite, finding yourself settling and starting jobs but never finishing them because short-term commitment is what feels safe to you. When people have quit on you your whole life, it's no wonder we learn to quit on ourselves. The same is true for someone who's had traumatic experiences in long-term relationships. Whether that be having been cheated on or left after years together. You may experience blocks and hesitation around long-term commitments, because of your fear of wasting time and energy, after having been burned personally in the past. It likely can make you feel trapped or burdened.

Once we've been able to make the connection between how we're allowing our past relationships and experiences to dictate our present, we're able to better control and manifest the future we desire. Whether that be in love, life, business, or claiming our status as a trendsetter in our industry, a self-made multi-millionaire, or a sex icon! Only by healing the dead-end blow jobs, one-night stands, weight gain, mom wounds, and feelings of being constantly taken from, are we able to truly heal ourselves and step into our flaming hotness across the board in life. Essentially, when we feel we've been ripped off, it forms blocks of resentment, anger, and a good old-fashioned pity party in all areas of connection. This shows up in four or more different forms. Time, money, food, and orgasms.

You may feel ripped off or scammed like time has been taken away from you, with kids, a husband, and household tasks to juggle. It may be that you're not making as much money as you think you deserve and feeling like an underappreciated workhorse over delivering constantly while never feeling compensated. It may be feeling like a lonely clit that's being neglected and ignored while you continue to spend your entire day performing as a mom, a wife, or a cum dumpster. Or a body that seems like no matter how many times you work out, or how many salads you eat, it never meets your standard, or gives you what you want, with hair that never grows, skin that never clears up, and the list goes on.

Let's say you have (or had) a pattern of choosing the wrong men. You recognize that you choose fuck boys or men who want you for sex and control. Why? What is it you like about these relationships? Personally, I would often find myself in bed with these men because I knew they worshiped my body. The steady stream of compliments they paid me on my ass, my boobs, my blowjobs, and my sexual performances, made me feel fucking amazing! They raved about being mind-blown by my reverse cowgirl moves, which to me, meant that I was successful. I was doing a good job.

After I lost weight for the first time, I went on a bit of a man-binge, and for a long time, I shamed myself for this part of my life. I recognize now that during this period, I was reclaiming my power, I just didn't realize it at the time. I set out to land guys that I knew the chubbier version of myself could never have attracted. I dominated the bar dance floors like nobody's business, basking in the knowledge that all eyes were on me. It felt like ultimate satisfaction. If I found out that a man had a girlfriend, I approached him as a challenge. I don't feel guilty about this part of my life anymore and I refuse to sit here trying to make myself feel bad for being 21 and experimenting with my freshly hot body. The power of my dark feminine breaking free and getting what she wanted felt amazing. Even writing about it now, I can feel my inner good girl rolling her eyes, and my inner bad girl beaming with pride.

I felt great in my body. Sexy, powerful, attractive, unstoppable. And, while the attention I received felt amazing, I still craved real love and genuine affection. When we feel underwhelmed in one area of our life, like our business, our body, or our passion, we often overcompensate and overperform in other areas. If you're feeling unseen, underfucked, or undervalued in your marriage or personal relationships, you'll be drawn to overperform at work, with friends, and with clients. Every time your husband rolls over and goes to sleep after sex, instead of telling you how beautiful and radiant you are, you're left with a feeling of void, which you seek to fill by signing a new client, gaining more followers on IG, or flirting with a stranger.

Actions taken from a place of intensity will only get us so far. While they'll definitely deliver results, those results are often temporary and fleeting. When we find ourselves in a pattern of needing to be angry, passionate, or desperate before we're able to move forward, the level of flaming bitch energy required for us to reach the next level will increase, which is exhausting and draining. Not to mention, not the healthiest of methods. I used to find myself in this pattern quite often. In order to grow my business, I needed to feel angry, so I would set about manifesting stupid people posting annoying shit on my social media feeds, slipping into my DM's, and sending me emails filled with their dumb opinions. I would then take these messages and either turn them into teachable moments for my audience, tell them to 'get fucked,' or say nothing, block them, and move on. But no matter how I chose to respond, or not, I needed these negative interactions in order to feel intensely enough for my business to grow.

Now though, I stand fully in my truth and am comfortable with being the villain at times. I've healed and accepted my inner bad girl so that I'm able to authentically embrace my gentle compassionate healing side, as well as my feisty dark side. The wholeness of my spirituality isn't always filled with love and light. I am who I am, and I'm no longer afraid to show her off. Don't dilute yourself, because someone will still hate that version of you anyway and they may as well hate you for who you actually are instead of who you're pretending to be. I'm willing to let people be mad at me if it means that I never have to be mad at myself for not being me. No matter how holy you are, you will always be somebody's villain.

The key is to always be a bitch faster and no matter the situation, keep your head high, your voice proud, and your best girlfriend on speed dial or power text.

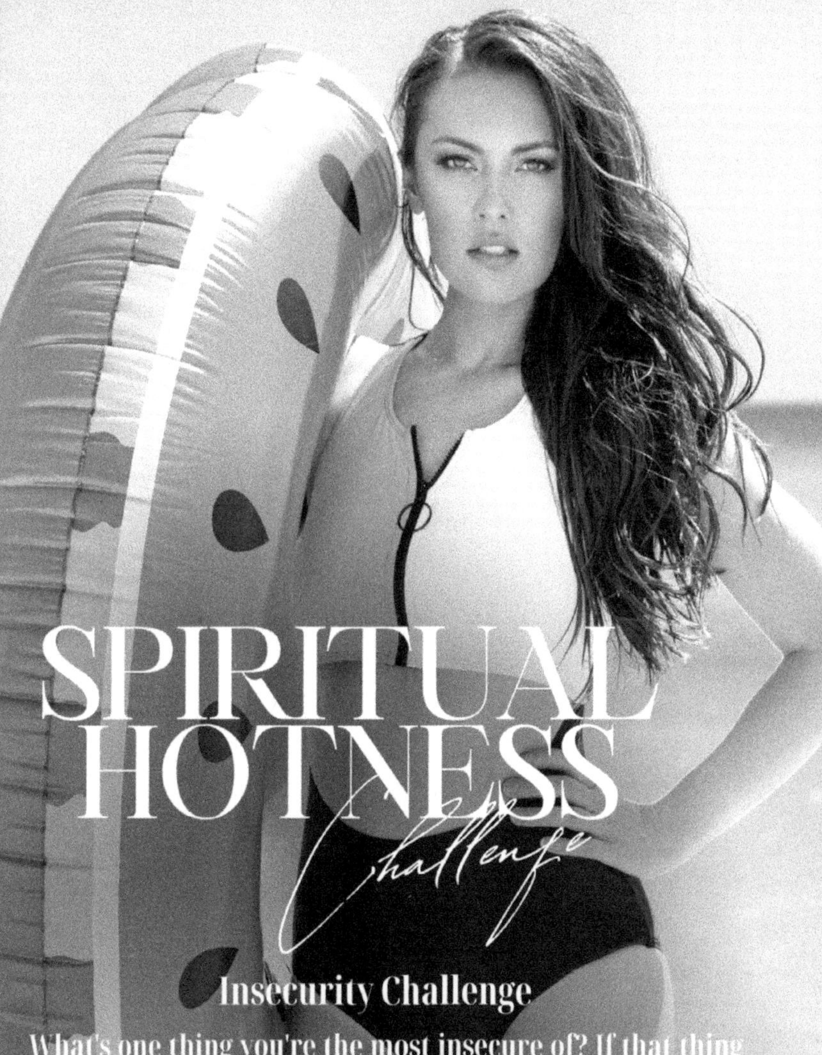

Insecurity Challenge

What's one thing you're the most insecure of? If that thing wasn't holding you back, what would you be doing differently right now? What would happen if you actually just did that thing anyways? What's one step you can take today, this Week, this month, and this year to build confidence in that area?

SPIRITUAL HOTNESS CHALLENGE

Picture yourself being bought something big and extravagant. Whether it be a dress, a dinner, a vacation or a piece of jewelry, you name it. Notice what your body does as you picture someone buying it for you without a single expectation back.

Gifts Challenge

PICTURE IS FROM MY 36TH BIRTHDAY PHOTOSHOOT DONE IN VANCOUVER B.C. WHEN I DECIDED TO PLAN MYSELF AN ENTIRE DREAM BIRTHDAY, JUST AFTER I GOT MY UPPER EYELID LIFT DONE

Notice any emotions and feelings that come up as it's being given to you. Ask your body where those feelings came from. If they're good feelings, say thank you, I welcome more! If they're not good feelings, picture your angels shining pink light on them and keep picturing it until you feel something different. You may have to this numerous times. If it's not working, ask your angels to show you another way.

CHAPTER 2

I SOLD MY SOUL FOR A PROMISE RING

"The day a man tells me what to wear is the day it ends. Never get between me and my dress"

I didn't actually have my first boyfriend until I was in my early 20s. We were together on and off for 4 years and at the time, I thought it was love. He cheated on me over and over and over again, treated me like crap, and was a grade-A fuck boy. Our relationship was a toxic cycle of breakups and makeups. At the time, everyone around us could see that it was an embarrassing and horrible situation. But I was under his spell, seeing only the good in him, continuing over and over again to choose pain and heartache over being alone. When I say that he was cheating on me, I do mean constantly. And he wasn't very good at it either. He'd get caught, deny it, scam his way back into my life and vagina - lather, rinse, repeat. If you're going to cheat, at least get better at not getting caught! It was during this relationship that I discovered and honed my investigative skills. Hacking passwords, figuring out the code to his landline mailbox, contacting the 'other girls,' and driving by his house and the local bar to check for his car. I'm not ashamed to admit my stalker skills, and I often brought friends with me for backup and moral support. Sometimes I would snot cry into the sleeve of their clothing, and other times we would throw things at his house. Nothing crazy enough to get arrested but enough for him to wonder which angry girlfriend was upset this time.

Every time we broke up, I would find myself feeling pity for him, his poor life choices, and his drug addiction issues. I desperately wanted to be the one that could heal him. It's so blatantly ridiculous looking back now, but it's just part of what you learn in your 20s. I can't tell you how many times, while doing my daily check of his voicemail messages, I would hear multiple girls thanking him for dates, where he'd taken them out with money that he'd told me he didn't have. I was his girlfriend and yet I was paying for everything because he never had any money. At least, he never had any money for me.

This is one of the reasons why I say that men and money are so connected. The way we receive love, sex, and orgasms from men is usually also the same way we receive money. We all have a code of values and standards that we live by, and we have patterns across the board in the ways we attract things into our lives. For example, as a kid, we never went out for dinner much, and if we did, we ordered water. Not juice or chocolate milk. This ties into feeling worthy of being taken out on a date, because usually that's what dates are. Restaurants and food. I simply wasn't used to being wined and dined as a kid which wasn't a bad thing. My dad was a hunter, so there was always some sort of home-cooked wild meat roasts and potatoes. I just wasn't used to dining out with my family, it was more thought of as a waste of money and so once I got older, I wasn't used to being taken out. Everything in our lives really is interconnected, whether we like it or not.

Fast forward to me finally breaking up with the douchebag cheating boyfriend. I eventually had to block his number, because I knew if I didn't, the pattern would continue. I didn't have the willpower to not answer his calls, so I removed that option from the equation entirely. I changed my environment and started to put myself through fuck boy rehab. I knew that nothing was holding me back from being the hottest thing he'd regret losing and I placed myself in the position to thrive. I joined a gym, set out to transform my body, and hired a personal trainer. I quickly lost 35 lbs. in less than 4 months. It's funny how when you let go of what's holding you back, you become exactly what you've always wanted. I wanted to become what every man wants. I wanted to be so hot that no man would ever let me go and they'd drop to their knees over my very existence. I paraded my new and improved skinnier body around loudly and proudly with every skimpy and scandalous outfit I could find. I wore every piece of fashion that I'd previously wished I could wear but knew I couldn't pull off. I felt glorious in my white ultra-low-rise jeans, Baby Phat tube top, hoop earrings, and stilettos. There was only one catch. Because my body transformation was completely driven by revenge, I wasn't truly healed from the inside. I changed my behaviors, but I didn't actually get to the root of all the hurt, betrayal, and anger. I was on a mission to prove everyone wrong about me, which would only continue to create challenge after challenge. I would conquer the challenge and prove everyone wrong, only to be met with another challenge, over, and over again. Prove, prove, prove. Fight, fight fight.

Instead of allowing a man to betray me again on such an intense level, I switched to dating the same sort of men, just slightly milder and more diluted. I call these patterns body betrayal blocks. These men were nicer to me and treated me better, but they were still inconsistent when it came to texting me back and making me a priority. Just to be clear, I wasn't receiving orgasms in any of these encounters - physical or spiritual. I was still selling myself short on so many levels, withholding from myself all the things I actually wanted which started showing up in my eating habits as occasional binge eating and ultimately sabotaging the body I'd worked so hard to create. Putting things that we know are hurting us into our bodies, whether it be a dick, a finger, or a weekend of overeating is a way for us to stir up more and more frustration, building until we reach the moment where we yell, 'FUCK IT,' and hate ourselves so much that we have no choice but to change. Every time we sacrifice what we actually want and break the promises we've made to ourselves to not settle or to do better next time, we betray our body's wants and needs. Now, I'm able to show up safely as my whole self, a boy mom, a sister, a wife, a lover, a healer, a psychic, a supermodel, a coach, a channeler, and a money-maker. It's only by fully expressing myself, that I've been able to make up for all the broken promises I made myself in the past, by becoming more whole and authentic than ever before. Never holding back, with a trail blazing behind me.

Back to that first boyfriend of mine. We met while I was working as a waitress, and he was a cook. If you've ever worked in a restaurant before, you know it's similar to high school where there are definitive clicks of the most "popular" people, and I felt at the time like he was THE guy. He was charismatic and funny, or so I thought, although looking back now I can't help but roll my eyes at my naivete.

At first, I didn't realize that I was only one of the many girlfriends he was entertaining. By the time I did find out, over and over again, I was so brainwashed and under the spell of self-punishment, that I convinced myself it was okay because I was still his top priority or the "main" girlfriend, not the side chick. I made up all these reasons in my mind as to why his lies must be true and denied myself the truth of what my own soul and every girl I met, was telling me. It still blows my mind how he was able to pull that off. I said to myself that it was okay that he was fucking around with other women, because he always came home to me, and took me to his parent's house, so I must be special or his favorite. It's funny and horrible how warped our idea of special treatment becomes. Even though he was cheating on me, over and over again, because I knew I was the "main" girlfriend, I was still getting to feel like I was being chosen and then every time I would catch him cheating, I would get to feel my own warped version of love where he would beg for me back. Looking back now, I think I was addicted to the feeling of him begging for me back, which made me feel needed and sought after.

At the time, I was so insecure in myself that I genuinely believed the idiot was the best I could do. I found out about his harem by doing some serious investigating. This was back when landlines were a thing, and I managed to sneakily watch through my side eye as he punched in his code to access his voicemail. When he left the room, I would dial in myself and hear messages from all of the other girls he was seeing. But even that undeniable proof wasn't enough to make me leave. How that was not enough is beyond me. One time after Halloween, I even found glitter in his bed for fuck sakes! He told me it was because they let down glitter from the ceiling at the bar and I later found out while on a phone call with his ex, that it was from her costume. You'd think that would be enough to leave right? Nope!!!!

Looking back now, I can see that I was brainwashed. I thought that if I was hotter, skinnier, or better in some way, I would finally be THE one. I hadn't yet formed my eating disorder, but this period was definitely where things began. It started with the comments he would make about other women and how fine they were, meanwhile, I was "cute." I had completely lost myself in a desire to be exactly what he wanted me to be. I changed my clothes to match his. I listened to his music, ate the foods he liked, and did things that he enjoyed. I remember telling myself that this was just how relationships were. We would get married because he loved me, and he would continue to cheat on me, but as long as I was the woman he came home to, it would be okay.

It wasn't until I realized that I was no longer his primary girlfriend that I decided to leave. How did I figure that out you may be wondering? Well, it was yet again my signature investigation moves. I stole his phone while he was sleeping and then extracted all the numbers I needed. Back then texting wasn't even a thing yet, so I stashed the numbers in my own phone to call his other girls. It was during one of those phone calls that it dawned on me, that I hadn't been his primary girlfriend for a very long time. While we were together, I paid for everything, telling myself that it was okay because it was a way for me to show him how much I cared. What I didn't know was that he was spending all of his money on his coke habit, and other girlfriends, wining and dining them, while I waited up for him to come home after the bar closed. Spoiler, there were more nights than I can remember where he didn't even make it home until the next day. At the end of the day, I stayed because I wanted to. I didn't actually want to break up with him all those times, I just did it because I thought I had to in order to get my message across and make a point, which I clearly could not stick to. It never works long term when we do things because we think we have to, you have to actually want to.

It was such a shit cycle of the same pattern on repeat, it was getting old and had the same outcome every time, except the highs weren't even high enough to keep me momentarily happy anymore. After 4 years of being in what I now refer to as a curse, I made the decision to leave. That's when I changed my phone number which was the first tool to breaking the curse. I took away the option to re-start the cycle.

Instead of mourning our failed relationship and the future I thought we would have, I funneled all of my anger, energy, and focus into transforming my body. I became obsessed with losing weight, toning up, and looking fucking hot. Instead of being addicted to him, I became addicted to the skinny. I changed my eating habits at first in a good way but then it became super obsessive and out of control. I reached a healthy goal weight but wanted more. I slowly started to cut out meals and snacks throughout the week in order to make up for my weekends of binging on beer, Denny's, and after-bar treats, all the while thoroughly enjoying being able to flaunt my newfound skinny-ness in every mini dress I could get my hands on. It was the first time in my life that I felt skinny, and I was soaking in every second of my whorey days and glory days. By restricting myself from food, genuine connection, and love, I developed a full-fledged eating disorder, I just didn't know it yet because I was too busy partying.

At the time, I didn't see any of this as being a problem, or unhealthy. I was young, had a banging body, and men lusted after me everywhere I went. I restricted my eating all week as well as working out more than was healthy, then binged on anything and everything I wanted on the weekends, and before I knew it, these benders became a regular occurrence and my free falling started to get excessive and out of hand, to the extent that I didn't get my period for 4-5 years, but it still didn't register in my brain that what I was doing was wrong. Most people are doing this on some scale, and honestly, this is how binge patterns start. Any time you feel out of control while eating and can't stop until you've eaten more than what you wanted to, that's usually a binge.

I spent my evenings in bars, drinking, flirting, and fighting in excess. I sought validation, attention, and affection and I was pretty good at getting it. I accepted dates while drunk only to feel disgusted when they showed up at my door the next night, but I felt obligated to go, after all, I'd made a commitment. You could literally call me the queen of beer goggles because of how drastically different things appeared to be in my head, versus the reality when they showed up on my doorstep to take me out. Of course, if they paid for dinner, I felt obligated to at least give them a guilt kiss goodnight, even if there was zero attraction and I had no desire to ever see them again.

I met my second boyfriend in my mid-20s. He was a nice guy and treated me like gold. I fell for him (or at least the idea of him) hard and fast, moving in with him after only a month. Within a few months, the honeymoon period was over, and I started to hate him, like really, really hate him. He was good on paper, in fact, he was perfect on paper. He was the polar opposite of my ex. He paid for everything, took care of me, was kind, loving, and genuinely treated me like a queen.

I'd never experienced that kind of attention before, and instead of basking in his adoration, I took advantage of him. For the first time, I had a man that was treating me like I'd always dreamed, but I used him and treated him like shit because unfortunately I was more attracted to what he stood for than the connection I had with him. Looking back, there were some other flags with boyfriend number 2, once again around alcohol, but it was hard to see them at the time because that was just what 20-year-olds did. Once I got used to having someone take care of me, it became normal and was no longer all that impressive. That initial connection wore off and I started to notice and focus on the annoying things about him. The traits that really started to turn me off and gross me out. I tried so hard to hang on to the relationship though, because rationally I had no reason to leave. It got to the point where he would put his hand on me, and I was so repulsed that I wanted to physically run away. Our body is talking to us all the time, and we are either listening or we're not. My body was literally rejecting him, but my mind couldn't get behind it. At least not yet.

After we'd been together for a few months, I started dropping serious hints about wanting a promise ring. I'd never had anyone buy me anything real before. Sure, they'd taken me out for dinners and drinks, and I'd gotten some necklaces, but never a ring. Again, it was all about the idea of it and what I felt it represented. Of course, because it was what I wanted, he bought me a ring. It was nothing crazy elaborate but for our age and where we were back then, it was good, it was real, and it was mine.

Despite his unwavering affection and the gifted promise ring, I was looking for a way out without admitting it to myself. We finally broke up on New Year's Eve. A girlfriend and I were getting ready to go out for the night and for some reason, he didn't like my outfit of choice. Specifically, I was wearing my signature look which at the time was a shirt, worn as a mini dress which just barely, and often didn't, cover my under cheeks, depending on the position I was in. My hair was dyed jet black, with side fringe bangs. I had silver eyeshadow dotted on the inner corners of my eyes and was sporting an oversized pair of hoop earrings. *(One thing you'll learn about me, ask me about any moment in my life, and I'll remember it according to the outfit I was wearing. It's a gift I have.)* I'd already been drinking, and finally had the balls to tell him it was over. Once again, I used alcohol as a permission slip to say and do the things I wouldn't allow myself to do while sober. Spiritually and emotionally, I had been checked out for a long time, but I'd stuck around and sold my soul, because I wanted that damned ring and a man who would take care of me so I could finally have an easy life.

It was about 3am and while everyone else was celebrating the start of a new year, my girlfriend was stuck witnessing the whole dramatic, outrageous scream-filled drunken breakup. She helped me shove all my clothes, with hangers, into garbage bags and we hauled them outside. Of course, being New Year's Eve, we had to make what seemed like a million calls and wait for hours before a cab could pick us up. It was horrible, but also a relief. I may have had to get wasted to do it, but I'd finally left, and it felt good. I never really addressed the real reasons I broke up with him, instead, I just pretended the final straw was his getting mad about me wearing that shirt dress with peek-a-boo under cheeks. I mean, that still would have been a deal-breaker for me. The day a man tells me what to wear is the day it ends. Never get between me and my dress. Not to mention, he stalked me for days afterward asking for the ring back until I finally gave it to him. It was not worth it ladies. What's that saying again? "*If you marry or date for money, you'll work for the rest of your life.*"

spiritual hotness challenge

Spiritual Nose Challenge

Picture someone you love, or like, or maybe even hate. Start using your spiritual nose to see what kinds of things you pick up when you smell their energy. Is it soft, spicy, musky, earthy, sweet? What do those scents mean to you? What do they represent? This is also a really interesting way to see how your body responds to these specific scents. I don't mean that you should actually go and smell their cologne, I mean smell their essence and their energy. It will tell you all sorts of secrets.

By the way, you can spiritually smell your own vagina, neck, hair, boobies, butthole...as well, but through the nose of your man. Try this. Pretend you are your husband, or your ex, or someone who has smelled your puss. Now, pretend you're going o town on your own vag, and experience it through the lens of them. Notice what thoughts and feelings come up for you. Pay close attention to the smell and observe if you translate it differently than how you translate the smell yourself. You can do the same thing with fucking. By pretending to be someone else, you can have sex with your own self - but as them. It may sound funny, but trust me when I say that I'm confident I know how it feels to spiritually fuck as a man, with a peen.

It feels warm, wet, inviting, and very primal. It feels much different and far less emotional than having sex as a woman. In my perspective I see it almost like experiencing an animalistic desire that's been programmed into their makeup as a part of their nature.

Memory Challenge

SPIRITUAL HOTNESS CHALLENGE

Find a memory from your past, maybe you're with a guy who you broke up with, or someone who never called you back. Go back to that moment, but as him. Almost picture yourself in his body and experience the whole experience through his eyes, his point of view, his perspective. It's pretty crazy what you'll realize. For example, I remember I had told myself this huge story about why certain guys didn't turn into boyfriends. In my mind it was because I wasn't hot enough or skinny enough, but when I went back to those scenarios and experienced them through their eyes, I was shocked to realize that those reasons had nothing to do with why we didn't work out. Many of them actually felt like they weren't good enough for me! But, you don't need to take my word for it, go ahead and experiment on your own. Of course every single person on the this planet is different and no matter what, you'll still be experiencing these memories with a slight tinge of your own perspective, because disconnecting from yourself completely isn't something you want to explore, but this practice will open up completely new ways of healing past traumas, and rewriting the stories you've told yourself that were never actually true.

CHAPTER 3

SMELL MY HEART

"Allowing someone to cheat on you, rationalizing it as acceptable behavior, just teaches you to start cheating yourself everywhere else"

I met my husband, Richard, while I was working as a waitress in a local pub. He'd become a regular, always seemed like a nice guy, and treated the staff with respect. All the other gals I worked with would whisper about him and thought he was a hunk, but Richard wasn't my usual type, in fact, he was the polar opposite of every guy I'd ever been attracted to. Once we did start talking, I found out that I was the opposite of his 'type' as well. Until we met, Richard was more attracted to the blonde, natural, make-up-free-faced, vanilla-type girl next door. And here I was, jet black hair, black eyeliner to the nines, smokey eyes, and not the girl next door. Basically, I was the enemy of the girl next door. I would have likely eaten her for breakfast back then with not an ounce of remorse. I was wearing black and grey tones, plaid flare pants with wedge heels, a black spaghetti strap tank, and had a large bump of backcombed hair for extra volume. When I ask him now, why he was attracted to me, he said that sometimes you don't know what you like until you see it. Oh, and that he liked my butt.

After seeing each other more than a few times in the restaurant, Richard decided to shoot his shot. It was music trivia night and he decided to name his team, '*I Wish I Was Tasha's Underpants.*' A name that was broadcast over the loudspeaker through the entire pub. Up until that point, we'd never actually spoken but I started to notice him more and more because of how much the other girls whispered about him. When I think about it

my biggest fan

now, I feel his angels were sending the whispers to me like secret little messages from his soul. This stunt though, got my attention, and as crazy as it sounds, it worked. Knowing him now, I see how on-brand it was for him, typical Richard using jokes to get himself into and out of things.

I found out later that Richard had been asking about me and was told by the other servers that he shouldn't waste his time. I was high maintenance and hated being asked out, especially for coffee dates. Maybe he saw me as a challenge, who knows? But he asked me out anyway and I said yes. Our first date was the dream date I didn't know I needed. He picked me up and took me for a ride on his newly purchased Harley. I want to point out here ladies, that our first date cost him zero dollars and we've been together over 16 years now. If I had some sort of rules around how a man needs to wine and dine me and chase me all over the city, we wouldn't be where we are today. I learned quickly that Richard didn't play games. He looked great on paper, was hunky, texted when he said he would, returned my calls, and didn't question me when I told him we weren't going to have sex until I said so. I remember being so surprised when I told him not to try to take my pants off and he listened which was the opposite of what I had been used to. My experiences with men so far had not prepared me for that - a man who respected me and what I said. I'd made a pact with myself that I wouldn't have sex with him for 3 dates, because I knew I liked him and wanted him to stick around.

Everything about Richard was new to me. He was 9 years older than I was, had a good job, a truck, and a house. He listened to me when I spoke and respected my decisions. When we did sleep together for the first time, after our third date, I spent the night with him, and literally never went home after that. Within a year we were talking about getting married, and Richard knew from the start that he wanted to put a baby in me. He'll probably deny it now, but I know that he wanted to knock me up immediately. Until then, I'd never seen myself as someone who needed or wanted to have kids, but after meeting Richard, I knew that he was going to be an amazing father, I never doubted that but still had my own concerns about my freedom and weight gain. Plus, I still wasn't getting my period and was knee-deep in a binge eating disorder that I didn't yet know I had.

Now that I'm thinking about it, Richard was the healthy version of what I had always wanted. When I was younger, maybe 13 or so, I remember fantasizing about being married to a biker guy and although Richard was far from a typical biker, what I was desiring was what a biker guy represented to me. Thrill, speed, and masculinity. Really, the motorcycle he rode was an attraction to being near the edge and the idea of potential danger. Before Richard, I had found thrills and edge through the danger of putting myself in situations that guaranteed my heart would be broken, over and over again. This was different, he was the healthy combination of attraction and love with speed but without any of the hurt and heartbreak. Our dreams and fantasies say a lot about what our souls are craving, and it's our job to fulfill those cravings and desires in healthy and nontoxic ways because fantasies are just the idea of something. They are not the same as the reality. You can interpret your fantasies the same way you interpret the dreams and nightmares you have while sleeping. It's all just your soul's way of bringing different experiences to light.

A fun activity you can do is to picture your favorite sexual fantasy for example. What position do you picture yourself in and what does that represent to you? How is the person you're with responding to your body and what's the environmental setting like? What does that represent to you? It says a lot about what your soul is craving to experience next. For example, let's say you're with someone having sex under a waterfall. He's lifting you up into the air and kissing your neck or whispering in your ear. This may mean that your soul's way of interpreting hot and steamy is being shown to you with the visual of a waterfall. It's a symbol of intimacy. Whether he's holding you up in the air making you feel light as a feather or taking you from behind making you feel submissive and taken, it's all just showing you the position you like to be in while receiving. This is also why our fantasies change because as our souls evolve, they need new experiences. Your soul may no longer want rough and tumble, throw-you-against-the-wall types of banging, it may want something softer and gentler. The way we connect during sex is the way we connect with many other things including money. Understanding the way we like to bang can go a long way. Another example is if you like to take it slow getting to know someone before jumping in bed and having a series of dates, you probably like to ease your way into most things. You likely enjoy trying things out and having a taste before fully committing. However, if you like to be more carefree and are easily able to feel good having a romp right away, you're most likely a fairly fly-by-the-seat-of-your-pants type of gal. This premise can work the opposite way as well and can be used to fill gaps. For example, if you love to be in control and in the power position at work, you may crave being submissive in bed. Everything we crave or feel disgusted by is an attempt by our soul to bring us back into balance. This is why I don't believe in sucking dicks if you don't want to. If I am not craving a dick in my mouth, there's a reason why. It varies with each relationship and its unique dynamics. This is why in one relationship you may be the world's #1 cock sucker and in the next you aren't. I have a whole set of guided meditations that will walk you through your body, money and sex fantasies and help you decipher what they mean. They come with journal prompts so that you can learn how to bring your fantasies into real life. They're called my "*Call Girl Mediations - become your richest hottest self*" and everyone who listens to them raves about how amazing they are.

My fantasies these days look different and honestly, don't really involve sex at all. Why? Because I'm sexually content and fulfilled (unless I'm going through another wave of sexual awakenings, which we will get to later). There's no real sense of craving for me sexually because nothing is lacking. I feel truly loved, desired, and connected. A craving for sex often occurs when something is missing or lacking in our lives, just like when your nutrition is out of balance, and you crave a certain food or nutrient. Of course, it can come from a place of love and connection as well, and this is why it's always good to just take a moment to ask yourself where it's coming from. The point is, that what we dream about in life changes and evolves, depending on what gaps there are in our unique life balance, what our priorities are, and whether or not we're seeking validation in a particular area. It doesn't always have to be for validation though, sometimes we want things just because they're fun, playful, and exciting. My current dream is for my husband and kids to surprise me with a poofy ball gown, a professional makeup artist and hair stylist on the ready, and a planned photoshoot with a picnic afterward to top it off. Basically, I want to be Pretty Woman, but without the hooker part. I think it's ridiculous that a woman only gets one day, her wedding day to have permission for a full day all about her and a dream dress, and that's why I have already decided that Richard and I will get married a couple more times or possibly even once a year. (We've already done it twice when I had a fully sponsored vow renewal). I don't need the whole wedding part, just me, him, the dress, and our kids.

Anyone who knows us, or has stalked my social media, can see that we're always having fun, laughing, enjoying each other, our boys, and the life we've created together. But my husband pretends not to be spiritual. It's funny because I know without hesitation that deep down, he is. Literally every human on the planet is a spiritual being. Some people simply explore it more than others, and some people express it more than others. Richard may not come home talking about a meditation breakthrough or a big epiphany he experienced at work, but I know that he feels a connection he can't explain when he goes snowmobiling, hunting, or hanging out with his buddies. Men may not always describe things as "spiritual," but trust me, they're feeling plenty of things, and just don't always say it, or know how to start talking about it. As women, we often judge our men for not growing or evolving, simply because they don't grow in the same ways as we do. Not everyone's spirituality is expressed in the same ways, so before you make assumptions that someone isn't spiritual or isn't evolving, take a moment to pause. I bet if you were to ask the right questions, you may be surprised at what you hear. Over the years, I've watched my husband go from a complete non-believer in the woo woo, to someone who surprises me with his gifts in miraculous and shocking ways. What most women crave is anything that forms a feeling of connection, but in new ways that aren't the same as their normal every day. For me, that's our spiritual evolution.

One afternoon I was sitting on Richard's lap, straddling him, while smushing my forehead and nose right up against him when I asked him to smell my heart, spiritually, and tell me what it smelled like. (I will teach you more about how to use your spiritual nose later, which is a great way to explore using your psychic gifts to connect to things, and you can do the same thing with taste.) I fully expected him to brush me off and pretend he had no idea what I was talking about, but without missing a beat he answered, and blew my damned mind. I truly thought I was going to drop dead on the spot when he explained what he meant. Have you ever watched a romantic movie and secretly pretended that YOU'RE the girl in the movie? Well, I felt like I was that girl. My husband had given me the ultimate compliment that I'd never known I wanted or needed. His one honest response meant so much more to me than our daily "I love you" texts, although I appreciate those as well. Richard told me that to him, my heart smells like bread because it's warm, inviting, and feeds his soul. He told me that being around my energy soothes him. And in that moment, I

our happy family

fell in love with him all over again. Why? Because he told me he loved me in a new way that I had never heard him say before.

When Richard and I first started talking about having kids, I was neck-deep in an eating disorder that I didn't know I had. I was in love, but still miserable. I remember thinking that having a baby might help. It seemed to make everyone else happy. We had only been together for a year when we started trying to get pregnant. I hadn't had a regular period in years but didn't think anything of it. Really it was just nice to not have to worry about leaking tampons, bloating, and the other annoyances that come with a monthly flow. Looking back now, I know that this was directly related to my eating disorder, but of course, hindsight is always 20-20.

When I didn't get pregnant right away, I made an appointment to see a doctor and make sure that everything up in there was okay. They put me on Clomid, which did nothing, and I was quickly informed that if I wanted to conceive, I needed to start fertility drugs and IVF. They made all these recommendations and diagnoses without ever asking about my nutrition or eating habits. I think it may have been because I was never overly big or overly small, I was always what people considered a normal weight, and people (even doctors) think that because your weight isn't alarming, there's no way you could have an eating disorder. We started the IVF treatments and life sucked. The entire process was horrible, cost thousands of dollars for the injections and flights to the clinic, and I still wasn't getting pregnant. After months of treatments and our first round of IVF, which wasn't taking well, I remember sitting in the doctor's office, waiting for my appointment to see how many follicles were growing. I'd picked up one of the magazines in their lobby and was drawn to an article about eating disorders. It included a graphic with a list of 10 signs that you have an eating disorder, and my heart stopped when I realized that I could check off every single box. I didn't tell Richard about what I'd discovered, but I did let him know that we should pull the plug on the IVF treatments and we both agreed to take a break.

It wasn't until we were talking with one of Richard's friends, a cardiologist, about how we were struggling to get pregnant, and I told him that my periods were basically non-existent. I was extremely healthy, working out all the time, and in, what I thought, was the best shape of my life. He asked if I had tried gaining weight, and I started bawling uncontrollably. In that moment we both knew that something was very wrong. He told me that my crying immediately after thinking about my weight was likely a sign that I should talk to someone. A specialist. So, there I was, talking with a man whom I'd just met for the first time, and within 2 seconds had asked me the right question that a fertility doctor hadn't taken the time, or even thought, to ask. It's crazy how the right medicine will find its way to you, and I see now how everything up until this point was adding up. Just remember, you can still be eating poorly even if you don't have an actual eating disorder. A lot of people will go all day long drinking coffee and skipping meals just because they're busy or stressed and that can be just as bad. As soon as we got home I literally Googled 'eating disorder clinics' and enrolled myself into counseling. That was when things really started to change for me.

Throughout my own healing process, I learned that when someone is first forming an eating disorder, there are a few key symptoms that most people have in common, the primary one being an obsession with food. For me, this meant thinking about food all day, every day. I never thought I had an eating disorder because I still ate, and I wasn't severely underweight. There's this assumption that if you have an eating disorder, you're either big or small. Trust me, that's absolute bullshit. Looking back now I can see that my own eating disorder first started with me skipping snacks, then I hyper-focused on the meals I was eating throughout the day, but still, the results weren't coming quickly enough. So, I started overcompensating (eating less and less while working out more and more) and cutting corners or bargaining with myself. I would tell myself if I was good Monday through Friday, then I could party all weekend. Some people call it a cheat day, to me it was a binge and restrict cycle that repeated weekly, and this is why I don't believe in having cheat days. Even the word cheat implies that you're doing something sneaky and bad. I believe in letting yourself have small portions of anything you want, every day if needed. When you give your body what it wants and needs, and you know how to balance, portion and pair your food together, you don't get cravings because your blood sugars are always stable and you're never neglecting yourself of anything. There were times when I would wake up in the middle of the night, craving food and I see now that my body was literally starving. I would plan out my binges, hiding any and all evidence of the choices I'd made because of the intense shame I felt.

It's kind of like when you backslide and fuck an ex. Sure, you might fight the desire or craving but you can only do that for so long before you give in and either take him back or let him into your bed for a night.

My therapist helped me to identify the root of my eating disorder as being that first cheating ex, my first love, although I wouldn't even call that real love. And while I didn't really believe her at the time, I see now how obvious it was that she was right. I also hired a nutritionist to help me begin healing my relationship with food, and within one year, I had my period back, like clockwork, and believe it or not, I realized that

I wasn't even ready for a baby. I'd been trying to get pregnant out of desperation to become happy. One thing I encourage you to ask yourself right now regarding whatever it is that you really want to happen, is what is the driving force behind this desire? You may be surprised at the answer you receive.

It's crazy, looking back now, to realize that by allowing myself to be cheated on, to see it as being acceptable behavior, I was saying that it was also okay to cheat myself. Every time I found out that he'd cheated on me, I would feel sadness, shame, and want to get revenge. The same held true with my eating, when I was cheating on myself, I felt sadness, shame, then revenge but instead of it being directed at someone else, it was all about me. So, remember this, the only reason people cheat on you is because you're cheating on yourself by being with them.

Overcoming my binge eating disorder was so much more brutal than just trying to get to my goal weight, but I did it and the second I felt confident in my abilities, I decided to become a personal trainer. Feeling like I was trapped in salad hell and a fat-burning obsession was something I knew I never wanted anyone else to have to suffer through, and I very quickly became known as the best personal trainer in town.

When Richard and I first got together I was still smoking occasionally and would do silly things like spraying perfume on myself so that he wouldn't smell the smoke. Of course, we all know this doesn't work. I would sneak out of bed, to the kitchen, to eat in the middle of the night, sure that he was fast asleep and had no idea about my midnight binges. Now, knowing him as well as I do, he's the lightest sleeper in the world, waking up if I breathe too loud in bed (he literally calls me Darth Vader when I sleep) so he most definitely was 100% awake and knew what I was doing. But he loved me anyway. In fact, he loved me before I was able to love myself. We should never have worked out together, because when we first met, I absolutely hated myself, but he loved me without question or hesitation and is still the biggest support on my healing journey. Even when I was a legit crazy person, packing my bathroom scale with me on a vacation to Mexico because I was that desperate to stay on track. The entire trip I was too scared to step foot on the scale though because I was eating meals that I couldn't control like I did at home. But that was then. Now, I eat intuitively most of the time, and other times I just eat whatever I feel like. My binge eating disorder is behind me, and nothing would ever be able to drive me to lose control and slip into a full-on binge and restrict cycle again. I'm a proud, doting mom to two amazing little boys, a business mogul with an empire that's growing every single day, in love with my husband more than ever before, and truly the healthiest and happiest I've ever been.

spiritual hotness challenge

Smell My Heart Challenge

First, ask someone to smell your heart & see what they say. You can also try smelling theirs or even your own. Second, tell your husband or friend that you love or appreciate them in a way you never have before. Give them a compliment by using descriptive words that are outside of your normal vocabulary. Maybe tell them what it feels like to be near them or have them in your life.

CONNECTION CHALLENGE

Imagine something in life that you'd like to connect with. This may be a plant, a person, an animal, or the wind. Close your eyes & allow yourself to feel their heartbeat, their pulse, their life energy. Then, sync your heartbeat, your breathing, with theirs. This is something that I practice with my husband, my children & with trees in the park to foster an even deeper truer connection than we've had before.

CHAPTER 4

PREGNANCY FELT LIKE A MOTHER FUCKIN SCAM

"The worst times have the best rewards, but it's your job to find those rewards"

Once I realized that the reason I was having a hard time getting pregnant was a much bigger issue than we'd initially thought and that I was actually dealing with a full-blown eating disorder, that's when I started meeting with a counselor, as well as a nutritionist. With their professional help and structure, I was able to recognize that my MO was to cycle from binging to withholding, and back again. It took nearly 5 years, but eventually, it clicked that I wasn't only binging & starving myself with food, and nutrition, but financially, sexually, and in basically every other area of my life.

For the longest time, all I could do was focus on getting my body where I wanted it to be, no matter what it took. The crazy thing is, everyone says, "*You've got to love yourself first before you're able to transform your body.*" But for me, it was the opposite. I was completely unable to love my body how it was. There were years when I genuinely hated my body and how I looked. It wasn't until I'd transformed my body into one that I liked that I could start to feel affection for who I was on a deeper level. I just knew that the extra weight didn't belong on me. Once I started to see results, I was able to appreciate where the results were going and fall in love with the changes I started to see. Spoiler though, just because you finally have the body you've always wanted, it doesn't mean you're going to be happy, or healthy long term, or even be able to maintain that weight. I was always happy when I was at a certain goal weight, but then as soon as I would see that number on the scale, I would treat myself to a binge, and without fail, go up a couple of pounds. As soon as that happened, it felt like a race to get the weight back off through restricting and over-exercising.

Again, I feel a lot of people do this, but some on a milder scale. Most people have a 10lb body fluctuation where they start to get plumper and then get back to gym and tighten up again, mine were accelerated cycles with the fluctuations bothering me and ruling my life. During this period, I was experiencing what I call 'human awakenings' all the time. They came in the form of breakdowns, crying fits, and time spent in my car blasting Spice Girls to desperately try and pull myself out of whatever pit I'd fallen into. I knew that what I was experiencing wasn't normal. I would constantly obsess about food. If we went to the movies, all I could think about throughout the entire film was the popcorn I wasn't going to allow myself to eat. I would make bargains with myself, that when I lost 10 pounds, I could come back and have some popcorn. Things began to spin even more out of control when I would start to anticipate and look forward to those binges. Fucked up right? I was craving the very thing that I knew was causing my torture. Again, this is what I call a curse pattern. My curse was a cycle that was happening through my relationship with food but it's a very common pattern in many women and can show up in all sorts of areas in life.

As women we also do this with spending and fucking. We can save up money, overspend, and then have to go back to working hard and hoarding money. Or even worse, keep overspending until debt stacks up so much that you have to keep chasing money and success just to keep up with your overspending. Fuck the guy until he hurts you, then swear off men and decide to focus on yourself. But soon enough you'll find yourself dick-binging in the arms of the same guy, with the same cock, and the same old story all over again, or maybe it's a different guy, but with the same old ending playing on repeat. Craving the very thing that we know is hurting us, because we can't handle not having that instant satisfaction. Eventually, the addiction gets stronger because, like any drug, the hits have to get larger to satisfy your needs. So, we need bigger or longer binges and before you know it, you're eating 3 chocolate bars in one sitting, or acting like your ex is the love of your life, when really, he's got a full-time girlfriend and 3 other side chicks, and you're the last priority on his list. Why? Because we're changing the habit, but not the feelings. We're cuttings things out of our lives when we really don't want to. The only time we'll truly be able to stop the cycle is when we've finally extracted the lesson and felt, understood, and released it from our bodies.

I remember very clearly, a specific moment at rock bottom, where I had already gotten to my goal weight, but I was still experiencing so much inner torture being a slave to my fat. I knew I wanted to stop being in diet hell, and right at that moment, I had a breakthrough where I realized the value of happiness. I said to myself, if I could just be fat and happy, I would be. Now, I know people get all mad at me for saying the word "fat" and even today I prefer to use the word juicy instead, but those were the exact words I heard in my head, and it was the moment that I realized that chasing the skinny wasn't worth it. I realized that if I could just surrender to who I was naturally, without stressing about what I saw in the mirror, put in my mouth, or the number on the scale, and be happy, I'd be okay. The crazy thing is that after I told myself this, it took the pressure off, which also made me stop restricting and therefore made me stop binging. Which in turn made me lose all my excess binge weight. I would call it my moment of surrender and acceptance that I could not do this fight with myself a day longer. Your body is not trying to punish you or work against you. It wants you to be happy and to have what you want.

After working with my therapist and nutritionist for a few months, I was able to quickly lose all of what I called my 'fluff weight.' And I'd done it simply by changing the way that I ate. There were still sensitive moments, I had to be very on top of my triggers, knowing what they were and being able to recognize them before I dove into a binge/withhold cycle. I developed a habit of being uber-vigilant with eating more frequently, not skipping meals, planning things out precisely, and preparing everything myself, to avoid any unplanned meal choices or binging temptations. One of the things that really helped me back then was to give myself a 100-calorie window every single day, to eat whatever it was I wanted. That gave me something to look forward to, instead of trying to anticipate a binge so that I could finally release pressure, this little trick allowed me a daily pressure release. I used the same concept when I quit smoking, I started at a pack a day, then cut back to half a pack, then back to three smokes a day, then two, then one, then half a smoke, and then in the end, a single drag. I just found that for me, knowing I could if I wanted to, was enough for me to get through.

Overcoming my eating disorder was difficult to manage, both personally and professionally. In my mind I would freak out in social situations if I had no control over the food and wasn't able to create a healthier alternative. I would get very irritable and on edge if I was expected to partake in whatever meal had been prepared by someone else. For example, one of my ultimate trigger meals was lasagna with garlic toast and Caesar salad. What's worse, is that this is one of the most common meals prepared when someone is hosting a dinner party, and there was absolutely no way for me to filter what was being put on my plate. Food addiction is a hard one because just like alcohol, it's everywhere and it really can't be avoided. Most people don't understand it, plus I wasn't telling anybody about it. Just like any addiction, there's a phase where you're still very vulnerable and can easily fall back into the cycle. In those first stages, it's important for you to have tools and environments that you know you can control. One of the things that I did to help me in group settings, was to bring a large dish of something tasty and healthy to share. Then I knew that no matter what, I'd be fine. People would understand that if I had just come out of rehab, you wouldn't serve me a platter of cocaine for dinner, right?!

These days I would never worry about a piece of lasagna ruining my life; however, I do still get irritated if I'm in a situation where I have no choice but to eat something shitty that I don't even want or like, just because I'm starving and there's nothing else available. Usually, it happens in airports when I'm stuck running in between layovers and all I can find is a day-old sandwich and I'm already annoyed because my flight was late which caused me to have to run as fast as I can down the hallway while wearing no bra. First-world problems, I know.

When I realized how great it felt to take control over my own health and wellness, I decided that I wanted to pursue becoming a personal trainer to help others do the same. I applied at our local gym, earned my certification, and things took off faster than I'd ever expected. At the time, I was working for the gym, meeting with new members to run through the complimentary consultation they received with their membership, and to everyone's surprise, I signed, no word of a lie, every fucking client that I met. I sold the shit out of those personal training sessions, with zero business training or sales coaching. Looking back now, I know I was channeling through my crown and out my heart chakra. My passion was sheer magic, and it landed for everyone. Without a plan, I would go into an entire motivational speaking session where I would get honest about the reasons why people don't succeed when they join a gym and how I could help them avoid those pitfalls. The gym's other trainers were dying to know what I was doing, obviously, I didn't tell them because I knew it was my own special thing. I kind of blow my own mind when I look back at how hard I worked and how above and beyond I was going for my clients. I would literally take them grocery shopping and teach them how to read labels, and what to put into their cart as well as create a whole personalized plan for them. I would text and email them in between our sessions and check over their food journals every time we met. The other trainers spent their sessions giving their clients a workout and expecting to see huge results. So, lame. I would say that I believe the workout itself is the literal least important piece of the puzzle.

Without even realizing what I was doing, I had basically turned my personal training sessions into life coaching with the addition of continued support on my days off, and outside of the gym for free. This was my first experience with coaching, and I still had a hard time believing that's what I was doing. To me, it just felt like I was talking to girlfriends, as I formed long-term relationships with all of them. My reputation online was growing, and I soon became the highest-paid personal trainer in town. Eventually, I made the decision to leave the gym because they weren't willing to work with me as far as my salary was concerned, and I set out to officially start my own business. I knew that the first thing I needed to do was secure somewhere with the equipment I'd need to meet with my clients one on one, but I didn't plan on doing it at the gym I'd just left. So, somehow within a couple of days, I had the idea while running, (which I now call a psychic download) to stop by the fanciest hotel in town and ask if I could pay them to rent their gym. They said why not and rented me their entire workout space for $30/month. I shit you not! My monthly overhead was a whopping $30, so everything else that I made from clients was money in the bank. There was no other way to look at it than that I was blessed, and it was meant to be. I know that my angels are guiding me every step of the way and sending me magical opportunities as I continue to hack my way through life without a stitch of college or business school.

My business was thriving, I had new clients signing up constantly and a 100% success rate. Everything was referral-based and word of mouth so there was no advertising or marketing to pay for. I shared my stories and tips on Facebook and watched the referrals come pouring in. My clients started to have huge body transformations at rapid speeds and that's when I took my brand further, turning my clients into what I call self-made supermodels. By this time, I myself was already being published and landing covers in various international magazines and I had decided I wanted to create experiences where my clients could feel like models themselves. I would take them shopping, style them, pick outfits, and send them to my favorite glam girls in town for hair and makeup. Then I would do photoshoots of them. I would give them modeling lessons where I taught them how to pose, move, smile, and flaunt their new bodies so that they would walk away feeling obsessed with themselves. I did all of that just because I wanted to and in turn, I became an incredible bikini photographer and went on to have multiple different bikini retreats. Some of my clients even went on to be published internationally in various fitness magazines themselves. You will never find another person who can do a Tasha Wall transformation like me, I guarantee you that. You can check out some of these self-made supermodel transformations on my website, so many amazing women in all different shapes and sizes, all flaunting what they've got without hesitation or apology.

When I found out that I was pregnant with my first son, I made the decision to move my business from the hotel gym to my home studio, that way I'd be able to cut out any unnecessary travel time, and my little nugget could hang out in his bounce seat while I worked out with my clients. As my services became more and more in demand, I raised my prices, and before I knew it, I'd gone from making $20/hour to $150/hour which back then felt like a dream. After I gave birth, I only took 6 days off work before I hopped back into things. It was amazing. My new baby made googley eyes at my clients and they'd fawn over him, we'd go running with him in the

pregnancy #1

stroller and I'd give them park workouts. He was such a good baby. I mistakenly assumed that the same would be true with our next child. Boy was I in for a surprise. I do sort of look back and wish that I had taken a little more time off just to connect together and be a mom, but overall, we had a good system going and it was a lot of fun. I needed that work time to stay connected to things that were important to me as an individual. I feel it helped me to stay grounded in my connection to myself and my body and it also gave me adult interaction time.

While I was pregnant, I was extremely conscious of not restricting what I ate, because I didn't want to fall back into my familiar cycle of binging and withholding. I ate whatever I wanted, but I also hated watching my body grow. It wasn't a fun thing for me. I was nauseous for basically the entire pregnancy. You know how they say it goes away after the first trimester, well my nausea lasted until around 6 months, and it was absolute hell. I couldn't stop eating because the only thing that kept the nausea away was constant food and McDonald's fries but even then, I would feel sick again within 20-30 mins. I could never actually throw up though, so I always just had this constant feeling of on the verge throw up. It made me so emotionally depressed, and I would cry all the time, waiting for the day he would come out so I could feel normal again. I also caught pneumonia in my final trimester with cough attacks from hell that kept me up all night. I just felt so ripped off when I would see all these women talking about how

mommy & me workouts

beautiful the experience was and seeing how happy they were, made me blind with anger and disappointment that I couldn't have the same thing. I felt like I'd been scammed and lied to about how amazing pregnancy was.

Looking back now as the more healed and woke version of myself, I know that I needed more rest. I continued to work out the entire pregnancy and I kept running until it was too uncomfortable, I know now that it was inflaming the nausea. If I would have been able to surrender to my body, it would have gone smoother, but the fear of extra weight gain kept me pushing just a little too much. I was so used to seeing all these women running marathons with their skinny little legs and arms and perfectly popped basketball stomachs, and I would compare myself to that not understanding why I couldn't be like them. Every single woman's body handles things differently depending on genetics, emotions, hormones and how easily they're able to give in to their growing baby. The faster you let the baby run the show, the easier your pregnancy will be. I ended up gaining 55 lbs., which took me about a year to lose.

After I gave birth to my youngest son, I planned on going back to work right away, like I'd done with his older brother, but that didn't work out very well. I got hit with bad postpartum depression, and no matter what I tried, he wouldn't stop crying. From the second he came out of my vagina until the day he started to crawl. It was a never-ending struggle between us. Me, wanting my freedom, and him wanting the same. Sometimes I find myself feeling sad now that I'm older, not sleep deprived, more aware, and have talked to so many women in different areas of spiritual birthing expertise, that I can clearly see now all the things that were going on and why my second baby was crying so much. First of all, he came flying out of my vagina so fast that the poor kid was in shock. He was born in 10 mins with a single push. There were no contractions and no long hours of pushing and resting. He just came blasting out into this world with one huge giant push. Let me tell you, I had both my babies naturally without any epidural or drugs, and faster is more painful. I have realized now that the way babies come out of the womb creates patterns for them. For example, my youngest came out so fast that to this day, he doesn't like to be rushed into things or put on the spot. He likes to be able to ease into something and have time to explore it at his own pace. He responds to pressure by shutting down. But, when he is in control, he loves to go fast on things like dirt bikes and quads. He really likes to control the speed at which he does things. I truly know and believe that this traces back to the trauma he experienced while blasting out my vagina in 10 mins without any real time for adaptation. When you really think about it, birthing in general must be such a scary and jarring experience for a baby.

My second son also wanted to be held, all the time. He wanted me to wrap him against my body all day long and walk around, never putting him down. That was the only way to calm him down, soothe him, or put him to sleep, but it made me feel so trapped and overwhelmed that the second he fell asleep I was desperate to put him down, and then he would start crying again. To get him to stop crying I would have to stand back up at 3am, wrap him tightly around my body, and walk around the house. I was not allowed to sit down in a rocking chair or lay down with him spooning me, otherwise he would purple scream. The only way we could make it work is that he would be wrapped tightly in one of those cloth carriers with his head to my chest, which also meant that his head wasn't showing, and our eyes weren't connecting. He didn't like to be rocked to sleep after breastfeeding either, which is normally when a mother gets to bond with and watch her baby fall asleep in her arms. We never experienced that together and I still get sad and emotional thinking about it, wishing I could go back and do it better. I feel so mean for wanting to put him down all the time when all he needed was my body and warmth to be present with him, I just could not see or think clearly at the time. All of this created a cycle of overwhelm for me and unsafety for him. I was doing the best and only thing I knew how to do at the time, and although I had an amazing midwife who explained to me that he was feeding off my stress, I heard what she was saying but I just couldn't receive it or change it. He wasn't one of those babies who would fall asleep in the car, in fact, he hated the car seat and stroller so much that he would also purple scream at the top of his lungs any time he was in one. It got to the point where every morning I would try to pump myself up for the car ride to drop my older son off at daycare, by holding crystals in my hands, and taking deep breaths while the baby would scream bloody murder in the back seat. Within a few months, my nervous system was shot. Plus add in a 2-year-old who would sometimes cry at the exact same time. Honestly, there are moments where I still can't believe we all survived. Our days started with a 45 min car ride of purple screaming and ended the same when we picked my older son up to come home. We repeated that cycle until my youngest could crawl. My whole body was in constant breakdown mode. If I had the chance to redo it, I would have done everything I could to surrender and dedicate my life and our first 3 months together to just holding him, creating a connection, and being his mother.

Now that I have a clear mind, I can see exactly what he needed, and I wish I could have had it in me to just give it to him. He was a poor helpless baby who needed me to be his safe place as he adjusted to life as a human, and he felt scared and trapped while going into his car seat. I should have just listened to his needs and let him create the flow instead of trying to be the one who created it. I was just so desperate to rush back to life and to have my body and freedom back, or even a few moments alone, I remember thinking, *"This is how Shaken Baby Syndrome happens."* I remember empathizing with the

me and Akio figuring it all out

countless other women who've dealt with postpartum depression (even though I didn't realize yet that was what I was experiencing), and fantasizing about throwing him out the window, just to make it stop. I also would shame myself, for not understanding how 16-year-olds and single moms could do *this*, meanwhile, here I am a grown-ass woman, with financial stability and a supportive husband and I somehow still can't get my shit together. I hid all of this from Richard and tried my best to put on a smiling face when he got home from work because I was embarrassed about the job I was doing. It was a dark time for both my baby and I. This entire experience also put an unexpected strain on my husband because the baby only wanted the tit and very strongly did not want a bottle, and the first time I finally left the house to have some space, I was only gone for an hour before I had to come back because he wouldn't drink any milk or stop crying.

I remember on one occasion that I got to a point where I knew I needed to walk away. So, I left him crying in his crib and went downstairs for just a few moments. When I came back upstairs, he'd been crying so hard that he'd developed a stress rash on his face which mortified me and traumatized us both.

For years after I would continue to get instant panic and anxiety any time, I would see a newborn baby or hear one crying, it would flash me right back into those tough moments in my life.

During this period my once thriving business tanked. I had no way of meeting with clients with my cup so depleted, and my relationship with my husband was suffering as well. He would come home from work and try to be helpful, washing dishes or folding the laundry and I would lash out at him because what I wanted was for him to take the fucking baby! Dishes to me would have been a huge break, and I found myself feeling resentful about what was expected of mothers in comparison to fathers. We fought all the time because he was genuinely trying to help, but it wasn't the kind of help that I desperately wanted and needed. The problem was that I was not communicating that to him and wasn't even in a space to be able to clearly figure out what I really needed from him and ask for it. I was forced to take the whole year off and lean on my husband financially, which was not in my plans and was my worst nightmare. Richard had zero issues with taking care of our family financially, but I'd gotten to a point where I based my own self-worth and value on 3 of my main strengths. The work I did, the money I brought in, and the body I had. All of which I felt had been ripped away from me. It wasn't until I took the baby in for his immunizations that I read a poster on the wall of the exam room that said, *"Do you have postpartum depression?"* And, as I skimmed through the list of symptoms, I started to accept that what I was feeling was normal. It wasn't just me, and I wasn't a failure or a horrible mom. Things finally started to turn around. It was a slow process, things didn't improve overnight but over the next 18 months, we slowly started to build each other back up and our youngest became happier once he started crawling. Over the next 3 years, we started to truly bond like mother and son and now with him being 6 years old, we have such a special relationship. I love him more than ever and I would never disregard his needs like that again.

How I handled that situation is my only regret as a mom and I have vowed to myself that I will never put myself or my children in a position to experience that regret again. I need to mention here too that I've never regretted anything in my entire existence before, so this is big for me. I will always be present with them and be there to listen to their needs until the day that I die, and I will never ever break that promise to myself. I can say now that I am so proud of the champion mom I've become and nothing else is more important to me than my family. I plan to keep my relationship with my kids as close as possible until the day that I die and continue, to become a champion grandma as well.

my boys

So, here's what I want to tell you out of all of this. It may, at times, feel as if you're being scammed out of something or losing some part of yourself, but you're not. You're actually just finding yourself. Feeling scammed is all just a sign that you're not fully in your power yet and it's your job to take that power back. The worst times have the best rewards at the end, but it's your job to find those rewards and to continue to stack them. It's always worth it and as of right now, I can say that motherhood is the easiest and most natural thing in my life because I have fully embraced, accepted, and fallen in love with the role and I'm lucky enough to have a hands-on husband who does the same.

About a year after my second son was born, while I was still in the depths of postpartum depression, and he was still screaming like a banshee, I decided that what I needed, like, really needed, was a photo shoot. (Now, I know this was also my way of doing a soul retrieval, which I'll get into more later.)

By this point, I'd gone more than a year without filling my own cup at all. My life had become all about surviving off the bare minimum, not to mention adjusting to being a one-income household instead of two. I booked myself a solo trip stopping first in Miami, Florida then sunny California, for 2 different photoshoots with my favorite photographers. It was going to be my first time leaving the family by myself and I was looking forward to being alone with pure silence. Something that only a mother can truly understand. It was a huge stretch for me financially and completely cleared out my savings account, but I knew this escape, this break, this reset was what I needed. I went all in with professional videographers, hair stylists, makeup, and the works.

The first shoot, in Miami, was all swimwear and was meant to capture my glamorous and juicy side. I wanted to highlight my body transformation since I had just lost all 55lbs of baby weight and I was ready to rebirth the new version of me. The second shoot was rawer and more natural, curated to authentically capture my depths and vulnerability. I not only posed for still photos but also recorded a video sharing my personal story about dealing with postpartum. Something I could share with other new moms who were going through the same experience, feeling lost, and alone. At the time, I was taking this trip, and posing for amazing photoshoots because I knew it was what I needed for myself. It was something that brought me joy, and I was in desperate need of a little joy. What I

photoshoot 1 yr post-partum with baby #2

didn't know, was that my soul was guiding me into and through the entire experience. Preparing me with hundreds of amazing new photos showing me, genuinely smiling, glowing, and feeling my best for the first of many self-published cookbooks, my new online transformation program, and the birth of an entirely new business.

Reflecting now, I'm able to recognize that I was channeling how to best market myself, my lifestyle, and my businesses, without having any real plan or idea that was what I was doing. The only thing I knew for certain was that I was re-claiming my beauty. After a year of crying together with my new baby, and walking around with 55lbs of extra weight, in a wet messy bun and no makeup, this was a huge treat for me. I'd worked hard, like really fucking hard, to uncover and fine-tune the new me. And you'd better believe she needed to be captured and documented.

It's crazy how things come together when we're following our purpose. I was finally feeling like myself again and in the best shape of my life, even better than before I'd had the boys. When I started sharing those professional videos and photos of myself online via social media, I would find myself crying tears of happiness. I was so proud of myself and all the trenches I'd muscled through. I realized then that what I was doing was creating an extension of myself, my personal life, into my own uniquely powerful brand. After that, without a coach, a business mentor, or any real idea of what I was doing, I created my first online program.

This is what I mean when I

say that business is either born into you or it's not. When the business you're starting is aligned with who you are, things will take off so quickly, and strongly that there is nothing that can stop the ideas and creations from pouring out of you. I hadn't worked in over a year, so my business funds were non-existent, and I couldn't afford to pay for professional help or coaching when it came to organizing, putting together, formatting, or publishing my first cookbook. So, I did what I always do. I figured it the fuck out. I Googled and YouTubed my way through the self-publishing process. I invented every single signature recipe after testing them out countless times with my own family, and I photographed and styled the food myself. I created a layout that felt right to me, then edited it, and got it online for purchase. I not only successfully self-published that first cookbook, but 2 others. (BTW, those 3 self-published cookbooks have brought in over $15,000 profit to date! Not bad for a business newbie.)

I decided I wanted to create a program with recorded workouts and life coaching videos to help other women lose 20lbs in 4 weeks. I did this by documenting my own journey, the workouts, and meals that I used to go back to my pre-baby weight while juggling a newborn and toddler. (This is now known as my *Runway Ready* program and is available on my website.) Looking back now, I realize that there are countless ways I could have made things easier and faster, but at the time, I had no clue and no help, so I created everything myself, from scratch. I figured out how to rebrand my website and create my budding empire on different platforms, which is a huge blessing now because I can still hop online at any time to change prices, programs, layouts, or photos. Here's the thing, a lot of people are so focused on their problems, assuming that they don't have the necessary resources, or that things have to be perfect and ultra-professional, but in reality, sometimes you just need to hack things together to get up and running. Then come back to iron it all out later. I can't stress enough how important it is to focus on what's important and take one step toward that goal every single day. Sometimes your steps will be tiny, and other days they'll feel like leaps, but as long as you're moving in the right direction, you're making progress. When I was creating that first cookbook, the tech side of things drove me absolutely nuts. Every night I would go to bed so badly wanting to quit, and every morning I would wake up and find myself working on it. Talk about sheer fucking willpower, determination, and divine guidance at its finest.

Five years later that first online course is still my signature program. This was when I really discovered the online coaching space for the first time and started thinking about money as a goal in my business. I started noticing how many online coaches were touting that they were millionaires, just by doing what I was doing. I hired my first mentor to help with taking what I'd already patched together and making it bigger. Then, I hired another mentor and another. It took about 3 years before I realized that while I was filling my cup by building my business and developing relationships with these other female entrepreneurs, I was emptying my bank account by investing in countless coaches, masterminds, and mentoring programs. The more money I made, the more I invested back into my business.

Before I knew it, instead of an eating disorder, I had a money disorder. It was the same fucking pattern. Instead of chasing the skinny, I was chasing the money. Instead of depleting my body of food and nutrition, I was depleting my bank accounts of money. It wasn't until I had removed myself from the vicious cycle that I was able to recognize how badly I was binge spending on self-development in order to feel special, again. I had wanted to feel special with a man, which I healed. I wanted to feel special in my body, which I healed. But when it came to feeling special among professional businesswomen and standing out as an industry specialist, I found myself addicted to self-development books, courses, programs, and coaches. I was addicted to chasing success but hadn't yet defined what success in business meant for me. When I was able to recognize my natural tendency to always feel things as intensely as possible, I was finally able to realize that the intense mind-blowing sensation I was chasing could be soothed just as well, if not better, by feelings of safety, security, sturdiness, and stability. I didn't have to white-knuckle it every month to bring in $30k in order to spend it all on a coach or program. I didn't need to pay for status, or a spot in the millionaire's club.

Looking back now, I realize that I was having what I call a human breakthrough. I've experienced both human and soul breakthroughs in the past, more on that later, but what sets them apart is that the human breakthrough is more of a surface-level solution. For example, I thought that I'd fully healed my issues around food, and my eating disorder, but I hadn't gotten to the root of the issue, so the same pattern and behaviors popped right back up in my business. While I loved the support, I was receiving from the sisterhood I was developing online, I realized that I didn't need to pay for that validation. My husband loves me, every part of me, the quirks, the boogers, the creativity, and the internationally recognized businesswoman I've become. When I started to focus on the ways I was receiving love, attention, validation, and support from the people in my life who were there because they knew me, like really knew me, my family, friends, and clients, I realized that I no longer needed to buy things for that fulfillment. It's crazy how we tell ourselves that we need an expensive bag, a big check, or a fancy life in order to feel like we're important, loved, and recognized. Especially in this day and age with social media, we over-consume content and get stuck in a never-ending loop of pointless rabbit holes, half of which are not even relevant to our soul's evolution and are just one big distraction.

I can clearly remember the exact moment when my human breakthrough happened. The realization hit me smack in the face. *I'm so sick of working this hard. I need this to be easier, and I can't keep doing things the way I have been. I'm fucking exhausted.*

I stopped seeking out external solutions and started focusing on my energy and gifts as a psychic healer. It was emotional and kind of hard at first, but it became easier over time. I connected genuinely and authentically with people on a soul level, people who spoke my language and related to who I am, and each time my gifts and psychic senses started to skyrocket even further. The stronger the connection I had with myself, and the more I healed within myself, the easier I could connect with others. Sometimes that connection is based on our kids, other times it's talking about husbands, ex-husbands, arguments, makeups, my future vision for you, your career choices, the threesome you had last night, or the sex you haven't had in years. Suddenly, my whole client roster was full of healing clients, and I had another newfound gift of channeling not only through my visions and messages but through my physical body as well.

When I'm reading people, my body constantly gives me signs and feelings, acting as a map for me to read and follow. For example, if someone is having stomach issues, I can channel into their body and feel the aches and cramps that they're experiencing, which helps me identify where it's coming from. Then I can scan other spots of the body to see what components are contributing to the aches and pains. If I get a pressure or swirling feeling in my head, I know that my client is currently feeling a lot of pressure or overthinking, and I can guide them through how to release those extra thoughts. If my client is having trouble opening her heart to a man, I can feel the wall up and the heaviness on her chest and heart and I can physically walk her through removing it. As my security, stability, and confidence have grown in my skills, gifts, and business, they have improved in my relationships with my husband, kids, and friends as well. And when I finally stopped chasing money, love, likes, comments, and validation, my emotions stabilized, and so did my finances. I stopped experiencing drastic fluctuations, and there were no more peaks and pits, no more feast and famine. I hadn't realized that all the pressure I'd been placing on myself for my entire life to work harder and be better, was desensitizing me. I could finally put down my sword and my shield of anger, and when I did that, my body woke up even more and I catapulted into what I consider to be my first sexual awakening.

The next program I created was *EXHALE* which is all about healing our relationship with the masculine. At the time, I was going through my first real sexual awakening, and feeling safer than I ever had before with men and money. I recognized the powerful codes and downloads I was receiving and knew I needed to share them with my clients. I started by teaching these via live videos with my clients but soon realized that there was no way I could personally connect with every single woman who needed to experience this healing. Just like that, *EXHALE* was born. Nowadays, many of my programs and courses are developed because of the questions I receive from my clients. By sharing with me the areas of their lives where they're seeking help, insight, and guidance, they're also tasking me with reassessing those areas of myself and my own life. I recognize now that my clients are always helping to heal me, just as I'm doing for them.

So, back to my first sexual awakening. It happened during what I like to call soul-fucking. Trust me, you want to read this part. One afternoon while talking with clients, I realized that one of my fantasies was to be taken. Not kidnapped or raped, but sexually taken, overpowered, and fully enjoyed by someone else. Now, I was home alone at the time, so I decided, why not live out my fantasy with myself? I laid down in bed and started masturbating. I imagined that I was being taken by a soul. Not a man, but by a man's essence, his innermost desires, and carnal needs. Over the next hour, I pleasured myself in a way I never had before, in a way I'd never experienced before, all while going through my ultimate fantasy. I tapped into that soul, pulled it up into my body, and climaxed. My clit continued pulsating for the rest of the day, and the codes I downloaded during that experience were powerful beyond what I'd ever experienced before. By taking myself through a good soul-fucking, I tapped into something I wouldn't ever want to do with another human, for fear of traumatizing myself.

That first sexual awakening absolutely blew my mind, and as they say, the first one is definitely the strongest. Suddenly, my root chakra, which is also the chakra for sexual energy btw, woke up. It had been locked up tight for so long, without my realizing it, and now I had this crazy huge sex drive that caught myself and my husband completely off guard. I started realizing that my inner bad girl had been struggling to achieve her high by trying to get something, chasing the skinny, the money, or the man. But now, I was able to take back my power. Control of my money, my body, my relationships, and my orgasms. Now, part of what I teach my clients is that they can experience their own personal fantasies anytime they want, whether it be with a celebrity, a stranger, their partner, or anyone else, all by taking themselves through a soul-fucking to unlock whatever codes their fantasies and desires have been trying to show them. Something men will never understand is that when a woman has an orgasm, we experience an indescribable spark. Galaxies open and our mind goes blank. It's a feeling of fully letting go, clarity, and surrendering to a state of pure bliss.

Before, sex had been something I enjoyed okay. But it was also something that I wanted to finish quickly. What can I say, I lost my virginity during a quickie in a bathroom stall. But now, I want sex to last as long as possible. When I'm with my husband, it can take hours and my orgasms spark through my entire body. These are what I like to call embodied orgasms, as opposed to surface orgasms. A surface orgasm is what most women are experiencing, and probably a key reason why many women feel their sex drive dwindling. But, an embodied orgasm, that's when you're connecting with your partner on a physical and soul level.

This was the same time when I started realizing that I no longer felt called to offer only one-hit-wonder programs, 3-day masterclasses, or 10-day packages. I stopped calling in only quickie clients because now I craved longer-term relationships with these women. When we have that aligned connection with our audience, with our clients, they don't need crazy flashing lights or over-the-top promo videos, because they see and feel that you're the real deal. As soon as I stopped looking for quick hits and made safety and longevity a priority, I started signing bigger, longer-term clients, putting money into savings, and having amazingly fulfilling sex with my husband. That's when I realized, I like my sex how I like my money. Attentive, consistent, and full-body orgasmic!

Want to know something funny? When I get a hit or download for a new course, service, or program that I want to create within my business, it's always out of a trauma response. And, without realizing it, this is just how I work. For example, when I had a bad breakup what did I do? Well, I lost the weight and became a personal trainer, successfully starting my first business. I had babies, was hit with post-partum depression, and wasn't sure there was ever going to be a light at the end of the tunnel, but I created a solution to help heal myself and others. Sadly, within our society and culture, it's 'normal' for people to have a horrible experience followed by a trauma response to sit and wallow in their pain. They aren't yet able to recognize their lived experiences as being a part of their story. A story that's still being written, and how the next chapter starts is completely up to them.

I get it though; I wasn't always this way. There were several years when I was pretty damn comfortable with the wallow. Now, I have my dream family, my dream body, my dream business, and my dream clients. I have all of that, and it's my core foundation, something so solid and unshakable that if I ever find myself feeling lost, I'm able to come back to that core. At the end of the day, all we really want in life is love. It's not that complicated, and it's the same for everyone, no matter our race, religion, background, or status. As a society, we often place celebrities, business moguls, and musicians on a pedestal, telling ourselves that they don't suffer from the same traumas as everyone else, as the general population, when in reality, at the root of things our traumas are very much the same, just like our goals, dreams, and aspirations. To be seen, heard, accepted, and loved for who we are. Trust me on this, I work with quite a few celebrities, and it really does always come back to love. *Spoiler: It's usually love for ourselves.*

Getting back to my passion for photoshoots and fashion, I currently have a designer endorsement with a high-end brand. Sounds amazing right?! It is. But what most people don't know is that I pitched myself for no less than 10 years to different brands. I wasn't doing it every single day of course, but I knew that this dream of mine was going to be a long game. I have an extremely low tolerance for people who want to complain about a three-day launch or are ready to throw in the towel when their genius idea hasn't worked out in a few weeks' time. There are certain people who stand out in life, it's those of us who just do what we say we're going to do. Sadly, most people don't.

When I first started pitching myself to magazines, I was super aggressive, which worked out well. I landed quite a few opportunities to be highlighted inside the publications, but not on the cover. I realized that to get a cover, you need to be represented by a modeling agency, and I wasn't getting picked up. So, I decided to be my own agent, to land my own covers. I was going to be a fucking model, no matter what anyone said.

I'll be honest though, that didn't last for long. It couldn't. I was putting so much of my time, energy, and focus into pitching myself to anyone and everyone, that when something didn't work out the way I wanted, I'd get really upset. It would hit me, hard. So, I took a break from the rat race and decided to start creating my own magazine to represent my brand. I got to be the cover girl every fucking month! Not only was I getting to do what I loved most, but I was also building a solid foundation for my business. Suddenly, I had energy to spare and was able to put myself out there in the modeling world in a more strategic and smart way. I guess you could say I'd grown up and was no longer just trying to pitch my physical transformation, but my story.

I realized quickly that the supermodel lifestyle didn't align with my own personal values. While I loved the idea of jet-setting around the globe for photo shoots in all the hottest fashions, I also knew there was no way I was going to move to LA, spend my days going to hundreds of open casting calls, or put off having a family of my own in hopes of achieving the dream. So, I continued modeling my way, scheduling my own shoots when and where I wanted, wearing what I wanted, and doing things my way.

If you're willing to work hard enough, you can achieve pretty much anything. But it's important to ask yourself, do you really want to work that hard? Sometimes it's worth it, but other times it's not. It's okay to decide that you aren't willing to work hard for something, that's a choice we each get to make for ourselves, our lives, and our businesses. For example, I get to ask myself, do I want to always be able to fit into my skinniest pair of jeans? Do I care that much about the number on the tag, or am I willing to wear means that are slightly bigger sometimes? Do I need to be at my skinniest every single day, or do I want to enjoy potato chips and pizza on occasion? I know what my answer is.

BIRTH CHALLENGE

Think back to your birth and how it went down. Think about your body and how it responded to the contractions and what your birth pattern was. Long and drawn out? Did you have time to prepare? Quick and easy? How does this relate to the way you handle things in life? Think about the position in which you gave birth and all the events leading up to it. What experiences, life events and emotions were you going through both alone and with your partner at the time of your pregnancy? How did you talk to yourself? How did you talk to your baby? How did your partner talk to you? All of these things were adding up and the baby was experiencing it all with you. How are these patterns showing up in your life today with yourself and your child?

spiritual hotness challenge

Spiritual hotness challenge

Motherhood Challenge

Call on your angels of motherhood & ask them what each individual child needs from you right now & why. Ask for one practical step or which specific practical steps need to be taken to change these & what emotional steps need to be taken to support this change. You can also ask for a vision of what the outcome will look like if this is consistently practiced. play with this in all relationships in your life both personal & professional, as well as your bank account.

CHAPTER 5

I SEE CUM FACES

"We all have the ability to explore our unique psychic gifts. Many people will have zero interest in doing so"

I genuinely believe that each of us has our own unique gifts and things we specifically can see. Some see dead people and can retrieve messages; some can see past lives or inner child versions of others. Me, I can literally see cum faces and naked bodies. I see naked people everywhere I go. When I walk around, I can often see flashes of images of people and what they look like nude as well as what they look like during orgasm. While it can be interesting at times, knowing that the stranger in line ahead of me at the store is circumcised, or if the woman beside me at the salon has inny lips or outie lips. The lower lips, not the ones on her face. My third eye allows me to see people at their most vulnerable, naked, and natural, as well as offering me a glimpse of what their orgasm looks like. Trust me, everyone cums differently. I used to get the visions uncontrollably but now I know how to manage my energy and my channels and turn them on and off. It can be extremely over-stimulating to see visions everywhere you go.

Of course, I didn't realize or recognize this gift right away. It wasn't until I stopped channeling from my head or my heart and moved my channel into the deepest part of myself, my hips. Why? Because the chakra at our hips is strong in sexual energy and this is why I can see cum faces because my sex chakra is open. Everyone is using their gifts from certain chakras, and the more evolved you become, the more you can utilize all your senses which brings out new and interesting things you can intuitively do or pick up on. Ideally, the goal is to be able to activate all our senses. When people channel from their heads they tend to be masters at thinking and mindset, and their gifts will be very intellectual. This will work to a certain extent, but what you think literally means nothing if it doesn't change how you feel. For example, you may be able to pinpoint thoughts that cause you to have anxiety, and you can try to switch those thoughts, but it doesn't actually address or resolve the root issue of your anxiety. It's only the top layer of healing. Of course, it always helps to understand your thinking, but most people can't just change their thoughts while in the middle of a spiral. Especially when those thoughts are one giant distraction from what's going on underneath and the feelings that are stuck inside your body. That's why I channel and read into the feelings from inside the body.

Each and every person possesses a different symbolic library depending on the way their specific gifts work, so this language, my language, isn't something that can be taught to anyone else. Instead, what I do is teach my clients how to understand their own ways of working and utilizing their unique spiritual gifts (which may not include visions at all). Personally, when these messages first started pouring in, they came at all hours and I had no way of controlling them, although they did seem to happen more frequently when I was running in nature. Now, I'm able to better control when I receive messages, turning my receiver on and off, to ensure that I'm able to protect my own energy and space. Setting aside dedicated time for myself and my family, without worrying about my psychic inbox filling up and distracting me from my own life. Think of it like a TV set or a radio station that you tune in and out of. Each person has a different channel. I now know the difference between a literal message and a metaphoric one, and I'm able to determine whether I'm channeling something from the past, present, or future. I've reached what I like to call my psychic maturity. I no longer need to use cards, crystals, or meditations to activate my gifts and channel messages. My body is the only tool I use to get my psychic juices flowing. Once I've tapped in and engaged my connection, the magic happens naturally.

Every one of us has the ability to explore our unique psychic gifts. Many people will have zero interest in doing so, while others will be born already knowing exactly what their gifts are, and how to use them. For example, you'll see kids who have been using their gift of voice and singing the most beautiful songs since they were 5. You'll also see professional athletes who are insanely gifted in their abilities and a huge part of that is because they naturally can sense with their bodies what moves to make next, combined with all the training they do to stay above the rest. Some people are born with it and naturally know what they need to do in order to keep growing, while for others their gifts will require time and energy to uncover and hone. The key to improving your own skills is to learn how to take the feelings and intuitive hits you receive and follow them deeper, using them as a roadmap, an asset, a tool to figure out things that you'd have no way of knowing otherwise. Most people will notice when they've experienced a sense or feeling but think nothing of it. For example, getting goosebumps or tingles when you see or hear something, that's your body giving you a message and most people just notice it and continue on. I've trained myself to have those types of feelings all the time and to use those feelings as a springboard to receive messages and insights for others.

One of my favorite things to work on with my clients is how to take their gifts, those feelings, and do something with them. In working with people at all different levels of psychic development, I've noticed that a lot of individuals, when they're first developing their intuition, experience it coming and going without warning. They don't yet know how to call on their intuition when they want to and turn it off when they'd like a little break. They just know that they sometimes have gut feelings, but they don't know how to get that feeling on command. This is a skill that isn't always the easiest to learn, but with patience and persistence, is very achievable.

In the beginning, I had to spend time meditating in order to find answers, now however, I can receive the answers I seek in only a few seconds, without ever having to reground or ask a question. When a client comes to me with a specific question, I usually have their answer immediately, if not before they've finished asking. No need to pull 30 Angel Cards, sage the room, or shove a crystal up my pussy. Because I've dedicated the time to exploring and understanding my gifts, my body has become the only tool I need. Nothing against those folks who like to use cards, candles, crystals, or any other form of spiritual tool, they are amazing tools to have, I simply view them as a way to kickstart your intuition. I've worked with countless talented psychics who continue to enjoy using Tarot in their readings, but because I've been able to harness the power of my body, those tools are no longer something I typically use.

One thing that a lot of people don't understand is that if you ask a psychic a general question, you're going to get a general answer. Psychics work off energy, so if you're all over the place and feeling scattered during your reading, chances are that the messages you receive will be scattered as well. So just remember this when you go into a reading, the better the questions, the juicer the answers. The power of a question is pretty amazing because you'll also actually find that once you can identify the question, the answer becomes obvious.

One of my signature gifts is being able to help people channel the ultimate version of themselves. The hottest, healthiest, sexiest, thriving, orgasmic version of who they are. But channeling that version of you isn't enough. I also channel the tangible steps for how they can get there. I never want to leave my clients with a vision of their future but no clue how to make it happen.

SPIRITUAL HOTNESS CHALLENGE

Fashion Challenge

Fashion is a form of color therapy. We tend to be drawn to wearing colors that align with our aura or how we're feeling inside. When we're thinking about becoming the person we want to be, we get to focus on channeling that new energy through the fashion choices we make. For example: A few months ago I found myself feeling blah, fat, out of shape, and uncomfortable in my body. I wasn't sure what was behind these feelings until I saw my reflection in the mirror and realized that the shirt I'd put on was one that I wore while I was pregnant with both of my boys. It was a baggy, oversized shirt that I associated with being pregnant, gaining weight, and feeling disconnected from my body.

When I was able to make this connection & change my clothes, my energy shifted immediately.
When you think about your ultimate self, what colors come to mind? What colors is she wearing? Reflect on the emotions and feelings you attach to these colors and imagine them as light moving through your body. Allow yourself to play with the intensity and vibrancy of these colors to find what feels best.

Color Challenge

Think about a decision you've been trying to make and the different options you currently have. Picture option A in one hand and option B in the other hand. Which one feels lighter? Which one glows brighter? If they had to have a color, what color would they be? What do those colors represent to you? Now ask your intuition what would happen if you went with choice a and what would happen if you went with choice B. See what comes up. It's your very first initial thought usually, don't second guess!

Spiritual Hotness ✦ *Challenge*

CHANNELING MY INNER CHER
2021

CHAPTER 6

ASK YOUR BUTTHOLE AND SEE IF IT PUCKERS

"You'll be singing my praises when you open a dialogue with your butthole and it reveals secret answers to you. I like to call this spiritual anal probing"

Society likes to tell us that if a woman has plastic surgery she's a certain kind of person, with certain priorities, morals, and lifestyle choices. There are many people who pursue plastic surgery because they want to be accepted, and don't believe that they can be as they are naturally. As for me, I have gotten plastic surgery not because I'm insecure, but because I'm vain. Because I want to, and I can. Life's too short to be spent not doing what feels right and fun.

I got Botox for the first time when I was 36 years old, and I absolutely hated it. I was so nervous that I fainted mid-procedure. Afterwards the doctor wouldn't let me drive home because it was too dangerous. His assistant went and got me snacks and juice to make sure there were no issues with my blood sugar and within a few minutes I felt fine, but they still wouldn't let me drive. So, I had to call Richard to come pick me up. The problem was that I hadn't told Richard what I was doing. I didn't want him to know that I was getting Botox - because I honestly just didn't want to hear his spiel about how I was beautiful as I was, I didn't need it, blah blah blah. SO, I told him that I was getting a pap smear and passed out. I knew that way he wasn't going to be asking any questions, and it worked. He picked me up, we drove home, and that was that. No questions asked. But I ended up hating the results of my Botox. I was frozen. I couldn't move my eyebrows, and all I could feel was this crazy amount of pressure in my forehead. The key to successful Botox is knowing what you want - a little movement or a frozen face - and starting small. I honestly don't know that I'd even necessarily wanted Botox at that time, I just felt like it was something I had to do in order to prevent myself from aging. I went through 2 doctors before I found my Dream Botox Doctor. After my first appointment, I went home looking like a stunned cunt. For my second appointment, the results were SO conservative that it was a waste of $600 and an afternoon. Finally, my third appointment, I knew that I really wanted the

Botox, and I realized that for my desired result, I needed a combination of things. Instead of going into my appointment basing what I wanted on my budget, I went in with pictures of what I loved, and what I hated on other women. I was still super scared about getting filler but looking at the before and after pics the doctor had, as well as my own reference materials, everything worked like a dream! My perfect Botox treatment is a combo of filler and Botox in a subtle way that isn't obvious to anyone else but is enough so that I feel fresh and rejuvenated. Richard knows that I get Botox now, and he hasn't had to pick me up from an appointment since.

Before I make an appointment for any kind of plastic surgery, no matter how small or large, I look at what's going on with myself, spiritually, emotionally, and physically. I always want to do as much as I can naturally, but there comes a certain point where some things can't be 'fixed' without a little help. In which case it's always nice to have a professional on speed dial. Anytime I'm contemplating a procedure I start by asking my body how it feels about having surgery. How does it feel about having Botox injected into it? Ideally, what we want to do in life is make sure our physical body and our soul are on the same page. Now, that doesn't mean that if your body says, "*Hell yes*" and your soul says, "*No thanks*," you have to listen to one over the other. But it's always best to ask. This same idea holds true for any urges we experience, from plastic surgery to weight loss, sleeping with a man, or deciding to shave your head ala 2007 Britney Spears. There's always a soul reason and a human reason behind these urges, we simply have to ask what they are and listen for the response. By asking our soul, "*What is it that you want to get out of this surgery?*" and, "*Is there another way to achieve this result without surgery*?" The same thing goes for asking, "*What is it that you want out of this avoidant or noncommittal man?*" And, "*Can you get that feeling elsewhere?*"

Too often, people bypass the spiritual and use plastic surgery as a band aid or quick fix for a deeper issue. And, if there's a lesson that you need to learn, maybe about self-acceptance, true beauty, or self-love, that you've side-stepped with surgery, it'll only pop back up in another area of your life or body and you'll just start wanting one surgery after another. This is where people experience something called surgery amnesia, where they begin to forget what they looked like before. Instead of reflecting back on who they were in the beginning, they begin comparing themselves to what they looked like before the last surgery. And, before they know it, they've completely lost themselves and feel a constant need to book another procedure and another, and another. Personally, I'm never trying to create a different image of myself when I opt to go under the knife, instead, I do it to maintain the image I've already done the work, physically and spiritually, to create. Plastic surgery can be a great option for helping us as women reclaim the pieces of ourselves that we may feel like we've lost as we've gotten older, had children, or changed our lifestyle.

I had a breast lift done with a super small implant. It was so small that it had to be custom-ordered and flown in on a private jet because the surgeon's office didn't carry implants that small. I did it because I wanted to have perky boobs and I felt I deserved that after all the time spent nursing my boys and putting in the work to transform my body three times over. I was fine with popping my mom-titties out

rockin my pre-boob job titties cleavage

and owning it, even though (before surgery) I referred to them as my beaver tails. To me, the breast lift was more about not settling for okay, and having exactly what I wanted, and nothing less. I never had what I'd consider nice boobs because in my chubbier days, they'd ballooned up to a DD, but as soon as I lost the weight the first time in my twenties, they deflated and became saggy. Having saggy boobs in my 20s before I'd even had kids seriously felt like the world's biggest rip-off. I deserve to wear backless dresses and deep-plunging tops with no bra and no sag. To this day, my boobs are the best thing I've ever purchased for myself. I spent years thinking about it and I went to my first consultation 6 years before even taking the plunge into what would be my first elective surgery.

I looked at boob pics online for months and months searching for the perfect set of dream tits. I knew I didn't want big honkers; I didn't want to go bigger, I just wanted them to be exactly the same size, except perfectly round and up higher. I didn't want an implant there at all, I was hoping to just have a lift in order to avoid adding a foreign object into my body, but the surgeon told me that my breast tissue was so soft that the lift would just fall back down within a year. Plus, I didn't have enough natural tissue to give volume at the top. So, we added in the tiniest implant that ever was, and I had him weight the exact size of the implant and then remove that amount of my natural tissue so that the size wouldn't go up. I walked out with the same size boobs. but better. They were a saggy B before, and a perfectly perky B after. In addition to that, I showed him the size I wanted my areolas to be, which was just slightly smaller as well.

After surgery, the recovery wasn't too bad, especially since I'd hired a private nurse to stay with me, make food, and bring me ice packs without having to worry about entertaining my kids for 3 whole days. I only had to take

Scan me for before & after boob pics

pain meds once during the entire recovery, and the worst part was honestly having to wear the stupid compression bra 24/7 and having to sleep on my back. It was worth it though, and now I refuse to wear bras as often as possible. They make me feel like I'm in boob jail and I need to break free and escape immediately. So basically, I walk around all day long with my nipple hard-ons, making people uncomfortable. I consider my nipples as one of my signature trademarks. They're long, like 3 Smarties long. I even debated having them trimmed down during my breast lift. Believe it or not, that's a thing. They just cut out a sliver, about mid-nip, then sew the tip back on, and ta-da!!! Shorter nips. I know, sounds ouchy right? That's why I didn't do it, plus my husband said no. When making the decision, I had a feeling that having my nips trimmed would diminish sensitivity, or maybe they wouldn't look quite the same. What if one healed crooked or gimpy? You really never know how your body will heal, so it was an easy no for me.

One thing that comes with any breast lift is the telltale scar tracing around the nipple and into an "anchor." Depending on the shade of your skin, that scar will vary in color, as well as how obvious it might be. Because I'm olive-toned and Asian, my scars typically turn purple before they start fading over the years. So, while I do have an obvious incision mark on my breasts, no one sees them except my husband, myself, a bunch of photographers, makeup artists, stylists, set assistants, all my friends, and anyone I happen to change in front of. What can I say, I'm not shy anymore. My husband doesn't care about the scars, my photographers touch up the incision marks before sending me the final prints, and at the end of the day I'm in love with my boobs. They're the perfect shape and size for me. My entire experience was amazing, from the first consultation to interactions with the staff, and as I mentioned earlier, the speedy healing time. The only reason I'm not sharing my doctor's name here is because he didn't pay me to do it - and that's just how I roll.

I also had an upper eyelid lift when I was 36. This means, they go into the crease of your eye and remove a small slit in order to open them up a little more. Again, the best thing I've ever done, although I was awake for the entire procedure with nothing but some numbing juice, and an Ativan which was frightening, to say the least. I could feel the blood trickle down the side of my face. This isn't something I'd recommend if you're squeamish. Again, my recovery was easy and pain-free, honestly, in a week or less I was able to go out and about in public.

Now, you're probably thinking, "*You look SO good Tasha, what if I get a botched job from a quack?!*" Well, that's always a possibility, I mean, accidents happen. But I've had great success with the pre-screening process I use to select my surgeons, doctors, and permanent beauty treatments. The first thing I do, after having that chat with my body and soul, is to look at the specific websites of multiple surgeons and surgery centers, paying close attention to the before and after photos of their clients. Honestly, this is something that I may do for a few weeks, a few months, or even a few years. Trust me, these are big decisions to make and not something that should be done spur of the moment. I check Google reviews and if possible. I try to talk to someone face to face about their experience. A great plastic surgeon is like any other artist. They have specific things they're most known for, as well as their own signature styles. Some are naturally more conservative, while others are bigger and bolder. Although I'm sure a well-trained professional is going to be capable of doing whatever it is you request, they just may not be the best person for the job. Also, if the receptionist is a bitch, it's a sign and I never go back or get anything done at that office. I believe that the staff is a reflection of who is running the business and I'm not fucking around with this shit.

I also rely heavily on my intuition. I mean, duh, right?! I knew right away when I decided that I was going to get a boob job that I wanted it to be with someone from out of town. But when I got my eyes done, I did that locally with a very conservative doctor who I trusted implicitly with my face. As I mentioned before, every procedure I've gotten has been for a subtle change. I never want to look like a different person, I just want to tweak things, so I look like me, only 5-10 years ago. I've had filler placed in my cheekbones, temples, and under my eyes. I also somewhat consistently get Botox injections for my crow's feet, forehead, and 11's. But you'd never look at me and think, *"Damn those are some big lips & cheeks!"* Not that there's anything wrong with that, you know I love a good Kardashian look, I just don't want to have the same lips, cheeks, butt, and frozen forehead as every IG model out there. My goal is always to look natural, not overdone. I sometimes take Botox breaks as well so that I can remember what I look like for real. Every so often, I will leave a couple of months where I just decide to love and accept my normal, nonfrozen face. I also do my own healing on myself which is something that I call "spiritual Botox." What that means is that I am constantly letting go of anything in my life that is old and not needed. The reason we do Botox in the first place is so that we can look young, youthful, and refreshed, and so in order to also feel like that energetically inside, we need to make sure that we are always welcoming in young, youthful (aka new) energy, because when we don't, we create what I call old hag energy. Old hag energy is resentful, pissy, and bitchy about her life. She's hanging onto old relationships, patterns, thoughts, and experiences that don't serve her, which essentially causes shitty feelings inside otherwise known as stress. Which also happens to be the number one sign and cause of aging. The more you hag, the more you sag. When I am working on myself and tapping to my most youthful self, I go into my cells and body, and I can naturally and spiritually start reorganizing my collagen and revitalizing my cells. I can spiritually run medicine through my face and my wrinkles to heal and detoxify anything that's wreaking havoc on my immune system and my inner glow. If that's something you want to learn how to do as well, you can always book one of my private sessions where we remove anything in the way of you being your most thriving and fresh self, both internally and externally. It's full-on awareness of yourself and the healing of your internal ecosystem. When your insides, your cells, your body, your brain, your hormones, your emotions, your relationships, your environment, and literally everything all around you, is working together and on the same page, that is complete spiritual Botox. We will also channel all the physical routines and products that will be the best for your specific beauty journey. Spiritual Botox means that we're not in a fight with ourselves over time. We aren't chasing youth, and we aren't running away from aging. We are practicing being present, but we also allow ourselves to do what the fuck we want to do. So, if that means adding some injections in, then so be it. If that means having a completely au natural look, so be it. I personally like to combine spiritual Botox with actual real Botox, but everyone has their own special balance. We're all going to get wrinkles one day, and if you plan to live a long time, you're going to get a lot of them. So, the faster you accept them, the less they will bug you and the more beautiful you will look to yourself and others. Inner glow is a real thing people!

One thing I recommend for anyone and everyone thinking about having surgery of some sort is to start flipping through magazines, looking online, and checking out profiles of people who have the look you want. Or the look you don't want. I typically book multiple consults and bring reference photos with me to the appointments. Before my boob job I collected pictures of my dream boobs, as well as photos of boobs that were way too big for my liking. Now, the reason for multiple consultations is easy. Just like when you're dating, there's something that happens when you meet someone online vs in person, and you can often tell right away if you like their vibe or not. I know I can tell within a few moments of interacting with someone whether I'm going to jive with them or not, and that matters a ton to me.

Another practice I have when I'm trying to decide between various different doctors is to ask my body what it wants, and I see how it responds. Quite often I'll drop into my body and ask my vagina, "*What do you think about this doctor?*" Yes, you heard me right, I inquire with my vagina because she knows what's up. I know that if my puss opens up and welcomes the idea, it's a go. But, if she closes up or gets crampy, it's a definite no. You can do this by asking any part of your body that you like or feel most connected with. Perhaps you want to ask your butthole and see if it puckers or if it relaxes. I'm not joking! Trust me, you'll be singing my praises when you open the dialogue, and your butthole reveals secret answers to you. I like to call this spiritual anal probing, because, why not. Don't forget you can reach a higher level and go deeper with your questions. If your puss or butthole are clenching, ask your body why. You can use this practice with any questions you have and test your body's reactions to see what it's trying to tell you. Like I always say, your body has the answer to everything. For example, think about someone you love and notice how your body responds. Where do you feel that love the most? What does it feel like? Then think of someone you loathe and notice the differences. I also use my third eye to picture the various options I'm entertaining, one in my left hand and one in my right and I notice if one option glows brighter in my mind, as well as what colors are connected to that choice, and what those colors mean to me. If it's a bad decision, I usually see an aura in my mind around that choice that has a sticky black and tar-like energy around it, or I experience a general foggy and heavy feeling. If it glows clear or is brightly colored and feels airy and light, it's usually a yes.

Now, I also have a whole spiritual process when it comes to making the final decision regarding a potential procedure. I start by running a psychic scan over myself, focusing on the specific results of this surgery. I use my third eye to scan for any short-term or long-term blips, as well as searching for any botches that could happen. I also ask my intuition to show me a vision of my results at 3 months, 6 months, 1 year, and then 10 years after surgery, and I request that my intuitive friends and healers do the same. Then, I write letters to my guides detailing for them how I want the entire experience to feel, from start to finish. I ask every single one of my angels to go and talk to the guides of anyone involved in my procedure, all the way from the receptionist to the nurses, and the surgeons. I write intentions about what I want to release as I step into my new eyes, new boobs, new skin, etc. I ask them to sanitize all the tools that will be used and run light grids through the surgical room as well as my body. Your angels and healing team are always there waiting for your instructions, all you have to do is tell them what you want. And don't be afraid to get super specific.

If I'm feeling especially nervous before a procedure, I call on my friends, asking that they do the same for me. Reaching out and contacting their guides and angels, for that additional support and protection. As with anything else in life, it's important to have people who can strengthen your connection in moments of doubt, and provide you with confirmations before, during, and after the healing process, because it's not always pleasant. Any time I have to be put under anesthesia, I experience a major case of the blues on the third day, when my body starts to come out of shock. Most people experience something similar, and it's important to have support when that happens. You may find yourself being consumed by irrational thoughts like, what if my husband doesn't love me after the change, and it's powerful to have loving and authentic support at those times. In the room right before I was put to sleep for my boob job, I was honestly sobbing and afraid that I was going to die, leaving my kids behind over a boob job. It felt very dramatic at the time, as well as when I look back on it now. What the doctors may not tell you is that it's the emotions that get you much more than any physical pain you may experience.

About 3 years after getting my breast implants, I started experiencing chronic fatigue and non-clarity as well as just this extra little bit of annoying fluff. I couldn't figure out what it was, but I knew that something was off. Everything that I normally would do to lose the fluff no longer worked, and the less I ate, the more I gained. I went to the doctor, and they ran a number of tests to check my hormones, my thyroid, my blood sugar, and everything else. But every single test came back normal. Richard told me that he felt like the issue was my implants. It's crazy how well he knows my body. Seriously, he can tell me exactly when I'm going to get my period each month, like clockwork, even before I start feeling any symptoms. So, I didn't immediately disregard his opinion, even though I really didn't want to hear it because I loved my tits! This kept going for months. I needed to take naps all the time, I felt over-stressed and completely drained. I knew deep down that the issue had to be related to my hormones.

I started asking my angels what was going on, as well as if it was something I was going to be able to heal naturally. Their answer was yes, which was a huge relief. Then, I reached out to my guides, asking them how I was going to heal myself, and their answer was the same, over, and over, and over again. *Rest. Stop running. Stop working out. Just walk.* So, I did. I stopped my regular workout routine. I stopped running for miles beside the highway. And I walked, at the park, for what felt like an eternity. I meditated and did healing on myself and my hormones every day, talking to them and guiding them on what to do and how to calm down. I realized while taking these slow, methodical steps that as an entrepreneur I'd gotten so used to always rushing, moving, and never having a day off, that I was living my entire life that way, without rest. I'd adapted to working small bits and posting during family vacations. It's something that I never saw as an issue, until I did. Something I know my fellow boss ladies will understand.

Every day, for months, I would check in with my guides to ask them what I needed to be doing that day, to heal myself. And their answer without fail was always to *rest*. This was an extremely frustrating period for me. Being told by medical professionals that there was nothing wrong with me, my hormones were fine, everything was good to go. But knowing with every cell of my being, that something was wrong. It wasn't until I was finally able to release my need to be busy, to be working, to be running, that I was able to hear my body telling me what I really needed. What we don't realize is that our bodies are constantly syncing up to the energy of our environments. So, when I was going for 10k runs alongside the highway, my environment was speeding vehicles. No stopping, no resting, no quiet, and not the freshest of air. But, when I started to walk in the park, I was surrounded by earth, by nature. And, as I was consciously making the effort to slow down my steps, my pace, I was already recalibrating my body to instead sync up with the natural flow of energy around me.

Slowly, I started getting downloads and guidance on what exact foods my guides wanted me to eat and none of it was the same as what I had been eating. After about 6 months, I finally felt like myself again. I'd been able to completely reset my body and my hormones. Just like that, I no longer felt guilty for taking a nap when I needed to, I no longer shamed myself for taking things slow and pausing to enjoy moments. I call this reset, Spiritual Discipline because oftentimes, not doing is just as hard as doing. Sometimes working less is just as hard as working more. For someone so used to working 24/7, it's just as hard to not.

The download I received from this experience was that too often, women are diagnosed as having Breast Implant Illness. And while I do agree, there are times that the root issue may be her breast implants, there are just as many, if not more instances where the issue isn't with the implants at all, but with an imbalance in her energy, her connection to self, and her connection to her environment. Our bodies are ecosystems, and when one thing is off, it affects every other part of us. The key is to see those effects as medicine. Everything is medicine, the flu that you catch, the headache that you feel, the weight that you gain. It's all medicine prompting you into exploring what the deeper issue is. Sure, you can pop a pill and mask the issue, but then it's bound to come back time and time again. Whereas if you're able to sync yourself back up to nature, have the right healing tools, and truly listen to the cues your body is providing, you'll be able to heal yourself naturally and long term.

Think of it this way. Sure, when something is added to our body, such as an implant, a piercing, a tattoo, a metal rod, or pins, it's going to impact our existing ecosystem. However, when someone needs to have a rod surgically inserted into their leg after an accident and they begin to feel those same effects I did, doctors don't immediately suggest that the rod be removed, they recommend that the person rest. Removing the rod that's now stabilizing the patient's leg isn't an option, so why then are we so quick to assume that it should be any different with breast implants?

When you really think about it, a woman's breasts are a symbol of nurturing. They're literally the part of our body that feeds and nourishes our children. So, when I realized that Richard may have been right all along, the issue was with my breasts, just not in the way he'd thought. I started healing my breasts, talking to them, and moving energy in them and through them and before you knew it, I was back in balance. Now I am able to help other women do the same, as hormones are so personal to each and every person, their cycle, their stress level, their genetics, and so many other things, they are finicky AF, you have to be so aware in constant connection with them. I am able to help people now intuitively discover exactly what their bodies want to eat and what they want to do for exercise in order to come back around and stabilize. And I teach you how to do it on your own as well so that you will always know what to do. It saves so much frustration from feeling like you're doing everything right and still not losing any weight at all, and I do this in my private 1:1 sessions.

PROCEDURE
CHALLENGE

Spiritual Hotness

CHALLENGE

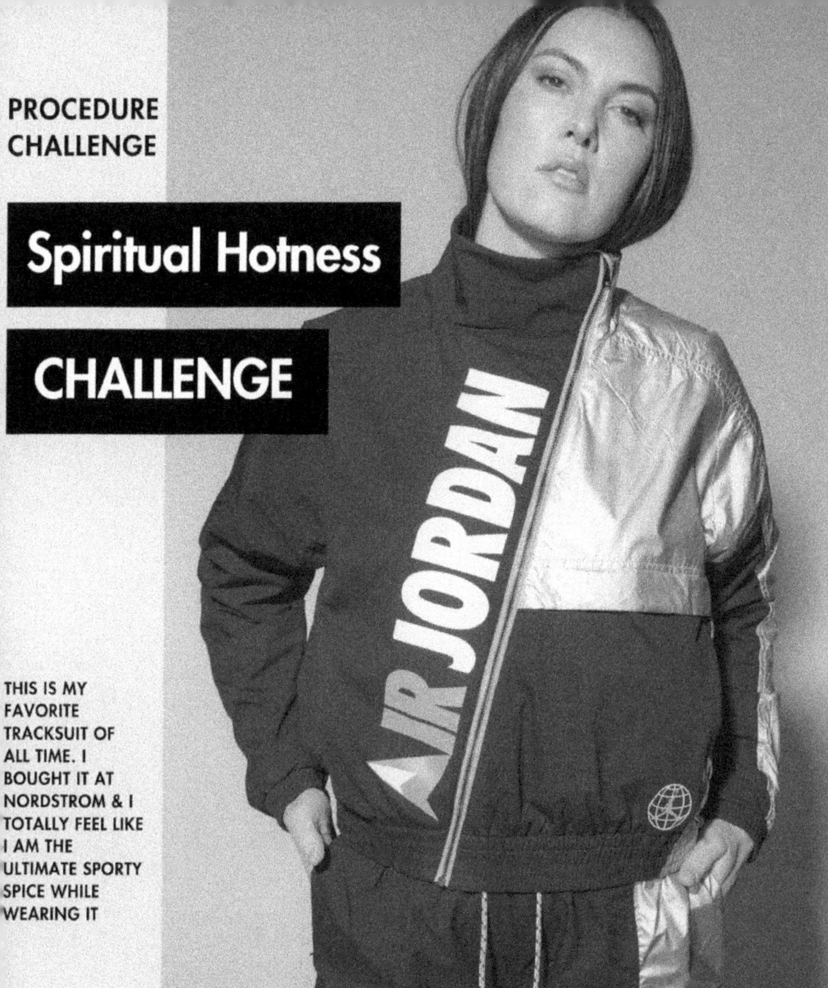

THIS IS MY FAVORITE TRACKSUIT OF ALL TIME. I BOUGHT IT AT NORDSTROM & I TOTALLY FEEL LIKE I AM THE ULTIMATE SPORTY SPICE WHILE WEARING IT

If you could have only one procedure done, what would you choose? Think about the physical end result & ask yourself what it is that you're craving from this experience? What other things might you be able to do, or bring into your life, to create that same energetic frequency in addition to, or in place of, the surgical procedure? For example; if your answer is Botox, to reduce the wrinkles on your face & feel more youthful, what other things can you do to experience those same feelings? Is there something in your youth that you feel robbed of, that you're attempting to regain?

SPIRITUAL HOTNESS CHALLENGE

Body Part Challenge

Find a spot on your body that you feel disconnected or discontented with. Ask this area of your body what needs to happen in order for you to fall in love with each other. Ask what this body part needs from you? What does this body part represent to you? What is its power and purpose? Remember that you're on the same team as your body – working together toward a common goal. Everything that happens to our body is a tiny miracle waiting to be discovered.

CHAPTER 7

MINDSET WORK IS OVERRATED

"No matter how full of shit a thought is, we can't change it until we've healed in the body. The only way past it, is through it"

You may see a lot on the internet about how 'mindset work' has become what many people think of as the one-stop solution to whatever ails you. But I call bullshit. Seriously, mindset work is overrated. I said what I said. If you're feeling offended, good. If you're curious about where I'm going with this, keep reading.

For many people, when they realize they want to make a change in their life, they start by changing their mindset and then pray that things integrate into their body, life, business, and relationships. As you've probably picked up from previous chapters, what I do is go straight to the body, before connecting to the mind. For example: Let's say that I'm picturing a trigger in my own life, a problem, or a block that I'm experiencing and want to overcome. Maybe the block is that I'm trying desperately to make more money in my career, and it just isn't happening. I feel like because I keep trying and failing, the obvious answer and truth is that I can't and will never be able to make more money. For those focusing on their mindset only, they'll start writing and regurgitating affirmations about how their dreams are possible. Maybe saying things out loud in the mirror or trying to think more positive thoughts. This isn't a bad thing, but the problem is that if you don't actually believe what you're saying, it does sweet fuck all no matter how many times you say it, trying to tell yourself to believe it. But for me, I drop into my body and tap into where I feel this belief, this assumption, this fictional story, in my body. What vibrations do I feel when I think the thought? Are they hot or cold? Soft or hard? Tingling or stabbing? Heavy or light? Then once I've observed that specific feeling and sensation, I picture myself making more money or whatever the thing is that I want to manifest. I see the money, whether it be physical cash in my hands, a notification on my phone, or watching as new clients jump into one of my many online courses. Then I allow myself to feel what new sensations develop in my body. Not emotions, vibrations. Emotions are sad, happy, scared, etc. Vibrations describe feelings like a racing of the heart, a pressure in the head, a flip in the stomach, a hotness on the face, etc. Once I feel it in my body, I focus on it until it changes, and I also start to notice what thoughts and visions come up as I stay in my body. By focusing on these feelings in my physical body, I'm able to attach better and understand what it is I'm desiring and manifesting, instead of just trying to think happy thoughts about it. Essentially, when I can tell I'm overthinking or spiraling into the wrong rabbit hole, I let my body lead the way and do the work for me because I trust it more than my head in times of overthinking.

This same practice works not only in your business, but your personal relationships, and more importantly, your sex! For so many years, before my husband and before I experienced my first sexual awakening, I initiated sex because I needed validation. I thought that sex was something that was expected at the end of a date or what I had to do to keep my douchebag, cheating, lame, not as hot as he thinks he is, boyfriend around. It was something that I felt was holding me and whatever guy I was seeing together, so I'd do my part, but genuinely disconnected from the entire act, more like a robotic thing that I sometimes would appreciate and have fun doing. Until that first sexual awakening (we covered this a few chapters back in case you missed it or want to read it again - it's pretty hot if I say so myself). Now, because I know exactly what it is that I want from sex. I know how it feels in my body, where I feel it, and how phenomenal it can be. My husband can literally put his hand on my boob or low back and my body responds by saying YES.

Funny story, my husband still thinks this is happening because I've reached 'that age,' where women start having a higher sex drive than men. In reality, though it's because, during that first sexual awakening, I went through massive healing that's allowed me to own and ask for exactly what I want. And, whenever we're arguing, he knows that my vagina locks up, we call it my frozen vagina, and no sex will be happening that night. Because it isn't something I want to do. No more going through the motions or checking things off a list. I have sex on my terms. I will say, I try to remember that the men in our lives are doing the best they can with what they know. Sometimes, as women, we have to go above and beyond, because we're blessed with just 'knowing' things before they catch up.

Since we're back on the topic of sex, let's talk about orgasms. We're all pretty familiar with run-of-the-mill orgasms that start in our clit, g-spot, or asshole, but not everyone is aware of or has experienced the power of a full-body orgasm - which has got to change. While most orgasms only last a few seconds or minutes, a full-body orgasm can last an entire day.

A full-body orgasm is a soul orgasm and happens when your whole body is alive, and you can feel the orgasm all the way from your head to your feet. Almost like doing magic mushrooms but without mushrooms and without peaks. More like consistent ecstasy through your entire body, tingling everywhere. Imagine being able to feel your heart beating in your legs and in your hips and in your everything. I know that for me, the more I am harmonized in my work/life/mom balance, the more I am able to have those full-body ecstasy moments. It's almost like, when you can achieve a life orgasm, oftentimes a whole-body orgasm will follow. At least for me, that's how it happened. It also comes when every piece of your life is aligned and fits. When you've achieved the body of your dreams, the husband or partner of your dreams, the family of your dreams, the career of your dreams, the wardrobe of your dreams, the bank account of your dreams - there are no missing pieces, none. A full-life-orgasm happens when you know that you've arrived, every part of your life feels connected and you know that you could die now and feel like you'd made it. That's when I felt like I could really calm the fuck down when I realized that I've already made it in life and there's nothing left to prove to anyone. And the more you can calm the fuck down and not be stressed, worried, overworked, and anxious, the better your chances are of having a full-body orgasm Think of it like going to get a pap smear. You can't allow anything in when you're all clamped up, embarrassed and tense. You have to stop fighting it and welcome it and there are certain people who make you clamp up more than others. It all depends on your previous interactions, arguments, dates, and compliments etc. For example, have you ever had your pap done by a not old at all, quite attractive man with good hair who low key reminds you of your husband? I don't recommend it. I'd more easily open up to woman or an old man who I care nothing about. Someone who's seen 50,000 other vaginas in his 70-year career. But sometimes you just got to get things over with.

I've personally mastered my own full-body and soul orgasm and am on a mission to help more women discover and achieve theirs. For a long time, years really, I knew that pieces of my life were missing, or not fitting how I'd like. Sometimes it was the money piece, I felt like I wasn't making enough, I didn't have the savings or emergency fund that I wanted, and I had to save up for several months in order to spoil my husband and kids with mind-blowing vacations. In the beginning years, the missing piece was in my relationships, both personal and romantic. There were also years when the missing piece was my body, how it looked and felt. When I look around me, I see a lot of people who possess things I want or would appreciate, but whose lives are still missing a piece or two. They might have a lot of money, but their family life may be suffering, or they have an amazing husband, but feel out of alignment with their mental and physical health.

You're probably wondering, *"Tasha, how the hell did you achieve the full package - that full body and soul orgasm?"* Well, as you may have guessed, it wasn't through mindset work. I dropped into my body and allowed myself to really feel, physically, how each of these perfectly aligned pieces felt. I asked myself, where in my body do I feel this desire, how does it feel, and finally, I pictured myself having achieved, obtained, or earned whatever piece it is that I'm focused on. I focus on the feeling of my dream financial status, my dream relationships, my dream husband, my dream business, my dream family, or my dream life, until it overrides anything shitty like fear, worry, anxiousness etc. I don't try to think my way out of negative loopholes because that just makes me angry and frustrated. There's nothing worse than thinking something shitty about yourself or another person while damn well knowing it's not actually even true, yet you can't stop obsessing about it. It causes more obsession. Before long, I began to feel those familiar feelings so much that I started to know the next steps to take, and I would get the most genius ideas of where to go next and exactly how to do it in order for my dreams to become a reality.

My strongest point of connection has always been my body, and it's when I allow my body to create answers for me – versus waiting for my mind to try & convince my body, that everything in my life aligns. It isn't until we take physical action that something becomes more tangible – only when a thought can create an actual feeling in your body, not an emotion, can you move closer to your actual desired result. There was definitely a period of time when I was focused on doing mindset work, after all, that's what many teachings tells us is the secret sauce to achieving everything we desire. But, when I was focused on my mindset, the results I saw were temporary. How many times a day do you have a thought that isn't beneficial to you, perhaps it's a limiting belief, negative self-talk, or a recollection of something a bully said to you in grade 3. We can try desperately to change our mind about something, but no matter how irrational or full of shit a thought is, we can't truly change it, or rewire it, until we have healed where the thought came from, which was probably decades back, and then dissolve it from the body. The only way past it, is through it.

Once I realized this and learned how to let my body and soul be the leading energy in my life, bringing my mind along for the ride, that's when I started experiencing larger and larger shifts. Our brains are here so we don't forget about things and its job is to warn us of any potential dangers, thank God for that. Our feelings, emotions, and actions, however, drive us to achieve results, which can then affect the way our brains work and process things.

When we change only the way we think about something, any underlying issues or hang-ups will simply move to another area of our lives. For example, maybe you're sick of being in diet hell and you can't handle being so hard on yourself about your weight so you decide that you will love and accept the way you are now. That's only works if it's how you truly feel. I believe in taking breathers when it becomes too much but we need to also be honest with ourselves. If you're just pretending to love your body because you're fed up and avoiding that fact that deep down underneath, you really want to change, then that is a much different story, and you need to find the perfect balance of a little bit of effort and a little bit of change. When we avoid, we end up spiritually bypassing and before long we'll find another spot in our life to feel crappy about. You can't get away from it until you fully learn the lesson of real self-acceptance.

When I started letting my body create my thoughts, that's when things in my life started to transform at lightning speed. It was through learning how to talk to my body and asking her for answers, instead of creating answers in my mind. This is another reason I believe so strongly in the importance of connecting to ourselves, because the information that we're reading on the internet may not be relevant at all to our unique lives. Some of my clients still like to use affirmations as a part of their daily routine, writing things down, taping them to the bathroom mirror, and speaking to them out loud. Even I like to talk to my guides out loud as I feel it helps solidify them, we just want to make sure we're taking those activities and combining them with body healing as well. I love being able to help my clients achieve the tangible results they desire most, not just a head full of happy thoughts.

NATURE CHALLENGE

Ask yourself what part of nature you feel most drawn & connected to. Instead of calibrating yourself to other people, focus on recalibrating yourself with nature. We don't judge the ocean for being bloated or at high tide, however, we judge ourselves when the ocean kicks up rocks, or we have pimples come to the surface. Spend a few quiet moments surrounded by nature and ask a tree, flower, or waterfall a question you'd like to receive clarity around. The key is to be patient, allowing the feelings, emotions, or sensations to provide you with an answer. Find ways to adjust the question you're asking, as well as what parts of nature you're communicating with.

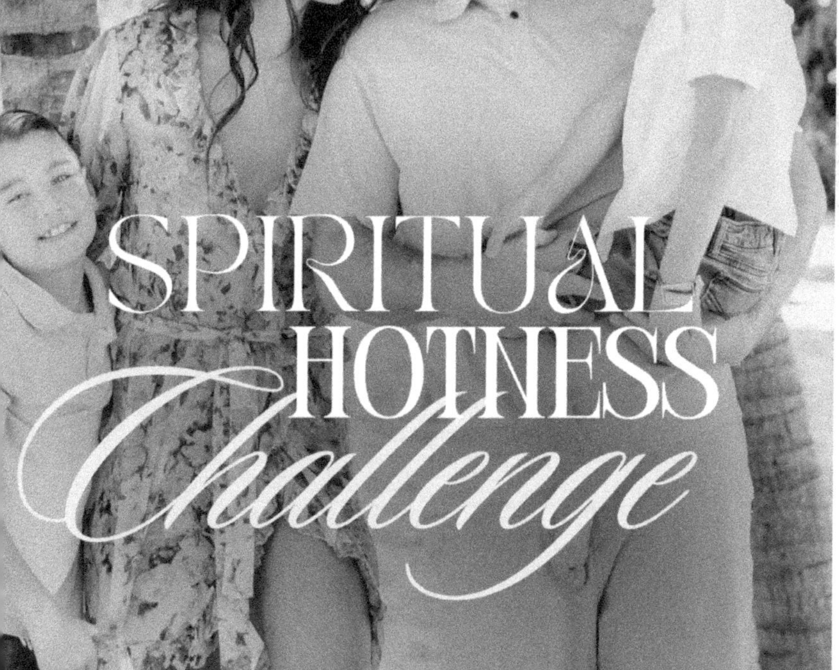

SPIRITUAL
HOTNESS

STUCKNESS CHALLENGE

Picture your stuckness as a locking box. you possess the key to unlock this box in your pocket & when you open the box what comes out? What emotions does it stir up in you? If you were to burn the box & walk away from it forever, if stuckness was no longer an option in your life, what would happen next? Where would you be going? what would you be doing? how would you feel? what would you be wearing? If there's no such thing as stuckness, where actually are you? What feelings are you actually experiencing that you're writing off as being stuck? What are you hiding from by claiming to be stuck? What's under the blanket? Ask yourself, What are you not taking accountability or ownership for? What is this really about for you personally?

CHALLENGE

Spiritual Bodyguard Challenge

Call on your Spiritual Bodyguard & ask them to create a bubble of light around you to keep out anything that isn't for your highest good. Create a list of the people & energies who are allowed in & who aren't. Choose a color that represents how you want to feel & imagine that being the color of your bubble of light. Think back to When a person has come into your life that you're unhappy with. call on your spiritual angel of clarity & ask them why this situation has come into your life, what it's trying to teach you & what it needs in order to change.

CHAPTER 8

I CAN BE A PETTY BITCH

“Dating a fuck boy is like trying to fit a penis into your belly button and expecting to love it”

One of the key reasons I set out to write this book was to authentically & vulnerably share parts of my chaotic journey so that other women who may still be holding back in their own lives might be inspired to say, "Fuck it," and just do the damned thing!

When we feel called to do something or to pursue a new path but hold back from taking action, we often tell ourselves that we're waiting until the time is right, the stars are aligned, and the weather is perfect. However, what we're really doing is allowing a whole lot of backed-up energy to build within us. Energy that will eventually need to be released as either a breakthrough or a breakdown. We make excuses to, and for ourselves. That we can't take action until we have all the answers and we've outlined the perfect plan. In reality, this only serves to foster mind fog, fear of failure, and a whole lot of self-sabotaging behaviors. It's important that we ask ourselves, *"Am I avoiding or preparing?"* And, *"What am I getting out of it?"* Usually, we avoid putting ourselves out there, or being seen, because it can be scary in the spotlight. It's one thing to wait until the time is right as you prepare, and it's another to procrastinate.

This same idea applies to our business and personal lives. Even when we're in the most seemingly perfect, committed relationship, there may still be underlying trauma holding us back from being our fully authentic selves, or really letting our partners in on a deeper level. Especially for women who are highly driven, it can seem like we always have to be 'on,' presenting the most engaging, hard-working, high-achieving version of ourselves at all times, so that we're never seen as having an off or grumpy day. And, if we let our mask slip, and show our not-so-shiny side, we'll be penalized for not being the perfect person we expect ourselves to be.

To avoid ever having to deal with this, I tell people right from the beginning what they can expect from a relationship with me because people only expect what you show them.

Those expectations will vary depending on whether we're pursuing a personal, professional, romantic, or friendly relationship, but what remains the same is that I'm not hiding anything about who I am. Another way that I focus on being 100% authentic is that I don't hype myself up, or force myself to act, feel, or present as being in an energy that I'm not because again, we train people what to expect from us. If I show up acting very proper and serious all the time, that's how people will expect me to be. If I only show one side of me, that's the side people will get to know and want. If I let myself be all the flavors of me, people will learn to either love or hate all the flavors of me. Seriously, it serves no one to pretend and it's very hard to maintain! If I'm on my period and I'm feeling pissy, I don't pretend that I'm not. I don't try to mask what's going on with a smokescreen of something that looks or sounds more pleasing. I've never once said that being the nice girl was my brand. So, get over it. Sorry, not sorry.

Truthfully, I find my own moments of sassiness funny, but that doesn't mean I don't also have moments where I question whether I'm being too polarizing, or wondering if I should have softened a blow. I'm still a work in progress like we all are, and one of the things I work on most often is grace, for myself and others. But even while working on being a more grace-filled person, I don't pretend to be love and light all the time because I'm fucking not. Even the most spiritual gurus have to put their garbage somewhere and let's face it, I can be a petty bitch. So often we think of healers, especially spiritual healers as being pure calm beings, floating on clouds, smelling like sunshine and rainbows. And I can be all those things, but I also fart, sometimes pick my nose, and am human, and flawed. Again, sorry, not sorry.

I think we can all agree that the fastest way for any of us to get what we want is to connect to it, right? So, if what you want is a man, the fastest way to get him is to look him dead in the eye and hold that connection. If you want a banging body, find pictures of the body you want, cut them out, and keep them in your purse, on your phone, or in the kitchen. Connect to that image, that feeling, that sexy AF reality. Trust me, it's that easy. But the other side of this is also being able to drop it like it's hot when you realize that what you thought you wanted, isn't good for you. Or simply isn't something you want anymore. Changing your mind about something doesn't mean you're failing. It simply means you're growing, shifting, maturing, and evolving.

For a long time, my goal was to be a famous model in print magazines and advertising campaigns. I worked on achieving that dream for quite literally, 20 years. But then, after devoting 20 years of my life to this one goal, I started to ask myself, do I really want to do all this insane work just to appear in one magazine, for one moment? Like a flash in the pan before I'm replaced with next month's cover girl. Or do I want to shift that dream, and create my own magazine, where I can be on the cover every fucking month! Neither option is better or worse, but my priorities changed from needing to be seen as being gorgeous and sexy AF by one professional creative director, to being seen as sexy AF by my own audience, my clients, my friends, and my family and myself. It all comes down to being honest with yourself about what you think you want, and what you really want. And not settling for a false sense of lust.

This past year has been all about looking, feeling, and conducting myself like a walking dream. Remember, we always have a human goal, or the thing we want to achieve, and we have a spiritual goal, the feeling we want to feel from that achievement. Our soul is wanting something out of every experience that we're craving and when something doesn't seem to be working, it's our job to look at what feeling we're trying to have by getting the thing, and then seeing where we can re-create that feeling in our lives. Whatever you're craving from a thing or a person, is always the thing you need to give yourself. So, if you want more likes, you need to learn to like yourself more. If you want more compliments, you need to compliment yourself, if you want your kids to calm down, you need to calm yourself down, if you want more money, you need to see your own worth.

So often in life, we think that when something doesn't work out for us, it's because we weren't hot enough, talented enough, good enough, or any other reason. But in reality, it's simply because we're not in alignment with that result. This holds true in business as well as our personal lives. For example, if your primary value is commitment, but the fuck boy you're dating values freedom above all else, there's no way a long-term relationship is going to work out because those values aren't aligned. It's like trying to fit a penis into your belly button and expecting to love it. Maybe some people can find a way to enjoy it, but overall, you can only go so far and so deep before something will need to change. Maybe he will change, maybe he won't, but you never want to go into a relationship falling in love with what you hope they will become. People do change, and actually I did not practice what I'm preaching at all because when Richard and I first met, I never wanted kids and he said he was never getting married. Somehow, here we are married with 2 kids and it's working, although that doesn't mean we haven't hit our fair share of speedbumps along the way. But, because we share the same values, priorities, and goals, we're able to pivot when necessary and continue on our path together. I think some of it is destiny but also our foundational beliefs and general lifestyle have always been aligned. True alignment to me feels natural, and easy, like not having to try, at least most of the time. It also feels like daily life. Like sitting on the couch together, for the most part, like laughing, farting, and accidentally eating your husband's toenail because he left it in the chip bowl. Who the fuck does that?!

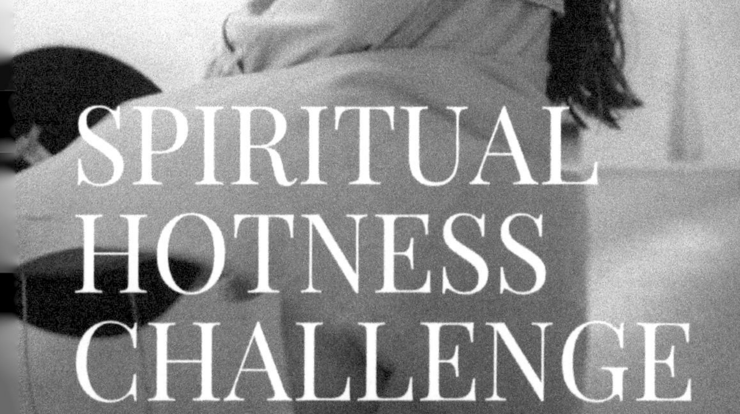

SPIRITUAL HOTNESS CHALLENGE

Power Challenge

Take a moment and think back to the first time you really went after what you wanted & got it!
When do you first remember looking at your reflection in the mirror and realizing, "DAMN I look good?"
When have you felt truly IN your power, like your passion had taken control? What happened? What responses did you receive? Were there any consequences? What did this teach you about yourself?

SPIRITUAL HOTNESS CHALLENGE

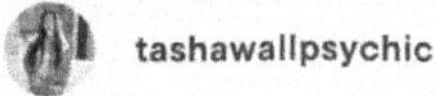

Conflict Challenge

sk yourself, right now, when was the first time a boy or
an made a comment about your cellulite, sexuality, the
smell of your vagina, color of your labia, size of your
ipples, or anything else that was negative about your
ody. Trace things back the moment you first erected
our own forcefield & ask yourself where that energy is
being stored as fat on your body?

spiritual hotness challenge

Self Sabotage Challenge

Think about one of your major self sabotaging patterns. Take yourself back to the very first interaction you had with this experience, situation, or substance. What were the series of events that lead up to it? What feelings were you avoiding? What was the environment like? How does this habit serve you & what are you getting out of it? How did you respond to the offending comment at the time? Did you shut down or get really loud & aggressive? What does this tell you about how you handle conflict? How is that comment still lingering with you today? I'm willing to bet that it's still there, hiding in your life but in a much sneakier form. While that one comment may not be showing up in your marriage, where you'd expect it to, it may be hindering your relationship with money or your career and causing you to either over compensate or under achieve.

CHAPTER 9

EVEN MY FUCK UPS ARE ON BRAND

"If you're going to do something, commit to doing it and don't apologize about it after"

Writing this book has been a profound healing and discovery process for me personally. It's crazy how when I focus on healing others, I wind up healing myself. As of this moment, one of the biggest downloads I've received through the writing process has been tapping into new ways that I can essentially rewrite my story. You're probably thinking, "*What the fuck does that even mean?*"

My standard method of healing, up until this point has been to focus on being completely present in order to untie the future. Being where you are is the fastest way to get to the next step of where you want to be because it's where your clarity comes from. You really can't see anything clearly when your chasing things or running away from them. Then, I follow up by tapping into the ultimate version of myself and channeling the various steps it will take in order to get there. This is what I like to call a "stairway to heaven," where you can see and feel the future you, but you also guide the present you, into her arms, creating a path and connection to merge these versions of yourself together in real life. A lot of people know how to dream, or they know where they want to go and what they want to do, but they feel overwhelmed by how they can make it happen. They have way too many ideas, blocks or thoughts spinning in their minds which causes confusion, overwhelm, or shut down. So, this is why it's so nice to have a new set of eyes on your purpose and clearing your crap because as humans, we get stuck in our clusterfucks and can't see the way out. What I help my clients do is clear their energy and their life in order to see the easiest next pathway. This means connecting to your soul's map, so that one step at a time we get you to your destination of total and complete fulfillment on both the inside and the out.

While writing this book, which has been like a huge, intense, journaling process, I've realized that I'm accessing a new way to manifest. By revisiting the experiences I've had in life, many of which I had forgotten about or glazed over previously, I've been able to see life lessons that I missed and have the most mind-blowing takeaways that I wasn't able to recognize at the time. It's been like rewatching a movie that you've seen before and noticing characters, situations, and lessons that you hadn't noticed during your previous viewing, being able to connect all the dots with each aha moment at a time. And, as they say, once you know something, you can't unknow it. This download has shown me new ways and tools to incorporate into my process. I've realized that when I write down my wishes, I can ask my body to follow. There's a stableness to this that I trust, as if I am deepening the trust of my mind and body connection like we are in the ultimate synchronization. Before I felt like it was more of a negotiation that I was doing. For example, when you can tell you're going into self-sabotage mode, that means that you and your brain are not on the same page, and sometimes it can even feel like you are enemies. This means you need to learn how to understand one another because two pieces of you are headed for messy and never-ending divorce. You have no choice but to come to some sort of understanding unless you want a never-ending battle. This is where healing comes in. As soon as you get on the same page with yourself, that's when you feel the full body YES to all your life decisions, and things skyrocket from there.

What many people don't recognize is the difference between masculine energy which is based around doing, achieving, and taking, and feminine energy, which is based on being, feeling and receiving. The key is for each of us to find a balance between the two. I'm naturally more of a masculine person. I'm very dedicated, disciplined, and consistent, which are powerful traits to possess. They allow me to stay very grounded in the here and now and they make me the queen of follow through and dependability. Over the years, I have been able to bring a ton more balance in with my feminine energy, which allows me to bring a little more flow in as well and has made it a lot easier for me to release control and let things come. One of the things that happens a lot with chronic overachievers (like my past self), is that they we are so goal oriented, that we will literally never stop and can become so obsessed and over focused that we can miss out on other opportunities and easier avenues that are right in front of our faces. I used to be so scared to be average that I literally could not rest because I thought it meant I was being lazy. Now I am so balanced in my life, and my biggest flex is my family and the lack of sacrificing I have to do in order to get what I want.

If I had to tell you a lesson that I wish I had learned easier, it's when you chase something, it runs away and you may get it for a moment, only to feel it slip right through your fingers again. Whatever you're chasing, trust me, you can live without it and that doesn't mean you will never have it. It just means, you're trying to get it in a way that is not maintainable. You need to recognize the signs for when you're getting distracted and chasing your tail over situations that would be easier to just let go of. For example, when you see an ex-boyfriend and for a second think, *"Maybe we should give things another try?"* Even though you have given it many, many tries. First off, NO! Second, you've been there, you've done that, and you know how the story goes. Or when you see a donut sitting on the table just after you've decided to eat better, and you know that you're going to feel guilty after you eat it. We've got to pick and choose what's worth it and what's not. Maybe there will be certain times that guy you're texting is a damn good bang, and maybe there will be times when the donut was worth every single bite. It's worth it as long as you don't feel guilty after. If you're going to do something, commit to doing it and don't apologize about it after. There's no point indulging in the treat when there's shame attached, that makes it a punishment and not a treat. We need to recognize what in our lives is treasure, and what in our lives is trash and don't let people and places pull you back into any dumpsters you've already climbed out of. There's nothing different in there then the last time. So, word to the wise, deal with your garbage before it turns you bitter, then dump it!

In most situations, people have to experience things for themselves, to learn whatever lesson it is they need. But, when they do have that shitty experience, don't give into your desire to hit them with an *"I told you so."* Whenever we feel the need to point out to someone that we warned them, and they didn't listen, it's a way for us to shame someone else. It's our attempt at soothing our own guilt and shame for experiencing that roadblock ourselves. Which serves no one and improves nothing.

While the past year has been one filled with personal growth and shifting, I also see and feel society shifting as a whole. The ways in which we buy things, consume knowledge and training, and communicate are all changing. We're being spammed with crap all fucking day, and we're tired of it. What so many big faceless corporations don't yet understand is that we aren't stupid. We as a society no longer want to be sold to, we desire a deeper connection. We want to feel something. We're moving out of the masculine and into the feminine, recognizing, addressing, and healing the ways that we respond to pressure, adrenaline, and stupid petty shit. We're realizing that what makes us different isn't what we can offer, it's who we are.

For me, this has meant a noticeable change in what triggers me and sets me off. In the past, a stupid comment from a troll online, hiding safely behind their keyboard, would have taken me from good girl to villain in 3 seconds flat. I lived for poking back at people, stirring up shit, and taunting them just to see their reaction. What can I say, there was never a dull moment and my goal in life was to fuck shit up. Now though, because of the work I've done to heal the traumas and experiences from my past, my inner bad girl has become less potent. She's found that love and compassion deliver the same feelings of fulfillment and satisfaction as a scrappy girl fight used to.

My purpose in life has shifted. I'm no longer the girl who seeks attention for my badassery, my no fucks given attitude, and my desire to be noticed. Now, I'm using my thirst-trapping ways for good. I capture attention with my confidence, my healing gifts, and I hold it by empowering other women to reawaken their own innate power. My days are spent helping other powerful females to heal their own masculine wounds and succeed in their lives, however that looks for them. My business has completely shifted as well. I'm no longer accepting that there's a limit to what I can accomplish. There is no glass ceiling. Sure, I'm going to fuck up, I'm still human. But I'll tell you this, even my fuckups are on brand.

As I move more & more into my calling as a celebrity healer, I still see myself creating courses & leading group programs in order to reach and support my clients, but it may look differently, as things change in life, business, and society. One part of my brand that will never change is my method of thirst-trapping people into healing themselves. Being able to grab your attention while reflecting back how you too can ultimately fix your shit.

This new year, this new phase in my life is all about surrendering and accepting support. Trust me when I say that if you have the money and funds to make your life easier, sweet mother of God, do it! Invest in the support, accept the help, and save yourself some time. If you don't, well then shut up and get to work. Asking for and accepting

support is something that's pretty damn hard for me because I'm so used to being in control of things. Knowing that everything is being done exactly how and when I want it to be because I'm the one doing it. But I know now that my foundation is strong. I know with confidence how every little piece of my business, and my brand, works and aligns with all of the other moving parts. I finally feel ready to allow other people to help support me in scaling and growing my brand so that I can continue helping to support even more powerhouse women to reawaken and reclaim their inner celebrity.

SPIRITUAL HOTNESS CHALLENGE

CHASE CHALLENGE

We get into loops where we're chasing thoughts & ideas (the hamster wheel of life). we're running away from someplace we don't want to be or chasing what we do want. Instead we need to come into the present. Sit where you are & notice which body part immediately comes to your attention.

Then, start to focus & bring your attention to that body part & notice what feeling you get when you focus. Even if you feeling nothing, nothing is still something. It may be boredom, stagnancy, emptiness or a disconnect.

Feel that feeling until something changes & that feeling becomes something else. For example: You may start off feeling tingly & move into a warm melty feeling. Ask yourself, what does the feeling represent to you & how is it showing up in your life today. The second that feeling changes, it means you've had a breakthrough.

Something's shifted tangibly, not just in your mind. Then ask yourself what's the new feeling & what does it represent in your life today, what actions will you need to take to support this change?

Imagine your truth & your authenticity is a big bright light super high in the heavens. Ask that bright light to show you the highest, most thriving version of yourself & then wait to see what you start to sense or feel. You may start to see pictures in your mind, colors, feelings or just sensations. Keep focusing, even if it's not clear right away. Try softening your gaze a little until you start to get more information & then continue asking the heavens, whatever questions you want to know in order to go deeper into the vision. For example: you can say, "show me what my typical day looks like" or "show me what my marriage looks like" or "show me where I'm working" & then, you can ask the heavens, "how did I get there?" & "what are three things I can work on now to get me closer to her?"

Spiritual

HOTNESS CHALLENGE

EXHALE CHALLENGE

ASK YOURSELF, HOW DO YOU LIKE TO EXPERIENCE OR RECEIVE DICK, SEX & WHAT IS THIS DESIRE TEACHING YOU ABOUT YOURSELF? WHAT WAS YOUR HOTTEST SEXUAL EXPERIENCE & WHAT MADE IT SO HOT? WAS IT A TOXIC OR HEALTHY COUPLING? HOW HAVE YOUR FANTASIES CHANGED & WHAT DOES THIS SAY ABOUT YOUR EVOLUTION? MY BEST AND MOST WELL-KNOWN PROGRAM, EXHALE, ADDRESSES THESE EXACT QUESTIONS, WHILE TEACHING YOU HOW TO PEEL BACK THE LAYERS OF YOUR SEX LIFE & EXPLORING HOW IT'S WORKING EITHER FOR OR AGAINST YOU. THROUGH THE MODULES, I TEACH YOU HOW TO HEAL ANYTHING THAT MIGHT BE STANDING IN THE WAY OF YOU BEING ABLE TO CONNECT NOT ONLY DURING SEX, BUT IN YOUR CAREER, WITH MONEY, WITH MEN & LIFE.

THANK YOUS

As this book comes to an end, I am a completely different woman than when I first started, and I know with confidence that while one chapter is closing, another is only beginning.

I want to thank everyone who participated in not only the making of this book, but the evolution of me.

Thank you to Michael Costello, Amanza and the entire glam team who helped me put this book cover together! Michael, you're such a generous, kind, and talented human. You've designed so many breathtaking dream dresses, and you truly went the distance to create the most special day I ever could have asked for. I know you're going to continue to do even bigger things than you've imagined possible! Amanza, thank you for always being the most raw and authentic human with the strength of a warrior and heart of an angel, and for bringing your energy and helping me sparkle with all of your styling techniques!

Michael Costello, Amanza & I

Thank you to my husband Richard, for being the most amazing man I've ever met and for loving me more than anyone else ever would. For rolling with all my crazy phases, even your least favorite phase where I leaked my own nudes onto the internet. Thank you for helping me bring our dream family into this world. I love you so much.

Thank you to my boys, Kai and Akio, for bringing me more happiness and balance than I could have ever imagined possible. For showing me the real meaning of life, purpose, and bringing out the best in me. I can't wait to see what strapping young men you grow up to be, and I promise to always check in and ask you how you're doing, even if one day you don't want me to. I can't wait to watch you grow and to also be the ultimate grandma one day!

Thank you to my dream team besties who have been there every step of the way since we were only 13, and all the other friends I've had beside me in various phases of life. All the way through the teenage years of road trips, breakups, makeups, and bar fights to the adult years of growing up, building families, getting married, and cheering one another on in our successes. I truly believe my friends of both my past and my present are the reason why I can sometimes get into trouble, but always just the right amount of trouble. Thanks for the undeniable trust and longevity and for being the epitome of ride or die. I cherish that, and I know how rare and special our connections are.

Milton Keynes UK
Ingram Content Group UK Ltd.
UKHW052136140124
436025UK00003BA/3